GENDER AND IDENTITY IN
CENTRAL AND EASTERN EUROPE

Of Related Interest

BEYOND STALINISM: COMMUNIST POLITICAL EVOLUTION
edited by Ronald J. Hill

THE SOVIET TRANSITION: FROM GORBACHEV TO YELTSIN
edited by Stephen White, Rita di Leo and Ottorino Cappelli

SOCIAL DEMOCRACY IN A POST-COMMUNIST EUROPE
edited by Michael Waller, Bruno Coppieters and Kris Deschouwer

POST-COMMUNISM AND THE MEDIA IN EASTERN EUROPE
edited by Patrick H. O'Neil

PARTIES, TRADE UNIONS AND SOCIETY IN EAST–CENTRAL EUROPE
edited by Michael Waller and Martin Myant

PARTY POLITICS IN POST-COMMUNIST RUSSIA
edited by John Löwenhardt

HUNGARY: THE POLITICS OF TRANSITION
edited by Terry Cox and Andy Furlong

Gender and Identity in Central and Eastern Europe

Edited by

CHRIS CORRIN

FRANK CASS
LONDON • PORTLAND, OR

First Published in 1999 in Great Britain by
FRANK CASS PUBLISHERS
Newbury House, 900 Eastern Avenue
London, IG2 7HH

and in the United States of America by
FRANK CASS PUBLISHERS
c/o ISBS
5804 N.E. Hassalo Street
Portland, Oregon, 97213-3644

Website: www.frankcass.com

British Library Cataloguing in Publication Data

Gender and identity in central and eastern Europe. – (The
  journal of communist studies and transition politics ; v.
  (15)
  1. Women – Europe, Eastern 2. Women – Former Soviet republics
  3. Sex role – Europe, Eastern 4. Sex role – Former Soviet
  republics 5. Feminism – Political aspects – Europe, Eastern
  6. Feminism – Political aspects – Former Soviet republics
  I. Corrin, Chris
  305.4'2'0947

  ISBN 0 7146 5033 1 (cloth)
  ISBN 0 7146 8087 7 (paper)

Library of Congress Cataloging-in-Publication Data

Gender and identity in Central and Eastern / edited by Chris
  Corrin.
      p. cm.
  "This group of studies first appeared in a special issue on
  'Gender and identity in Central and Eastern Europe' of The journal
  of communist studies and transition politics (ISSN 1352-3279)
  published by Frank Cass" – P. [   ].
  Includes bibliographical references (p.   ) and index.
  ISBN 0-7146-5033-1 (cloth). – ISBN 0-7146-8087-7 (pbk.)
  1. Women–Europe, Eastern–Social conditions. 2. Women–Europe,
  Central–Social conditions. 3. Women in politics–Europe, Eastern.
  4. Women in politics–Europe, Central. I. Corrin, Chris, 1956–   .
  II. Journal of communist studies and transition politics.
  HQ1590.7.G45   1999
  305.42'0940dc21   99-17015
                                                                  CIP

This group of studies first appeared in a Special Issue on
'Gender and Identity in Central and Eastern Europe'
of *The Journal of Communist Studies and Transition Politics* (ISSN 1352-3279)
15/1 (March 1999) published by Frank Cass.

Printed in Great Britain by Antony Rowe Ltd., Chippenham, Wiltshire

Contents

Gender and Identity in Central and Eastern Europe

CHRIS CORRIN

The transitional changes which societies in Central and Eastern Europe have been undergoing for a decade since the collapse of the 'Soviet empire' have had far-reaching effects on the lives of their citizens. Changes and continuities are apparent in various spheres, and this special issue considers the cross-cutting influences of gender and identity in the ways in which various changes are experienced and influenced. It has long been recognized that women are agents of change and yet suffer as 'victims' in some of the post-Soviet moves from state socialist systems to new societies with multi-party democracies and developing market economies.

Early studies in this area had a focus on recognizing the realities of 'actually existing socialism' within a gendered analysis of change, equality and difference and the choices (or lack of them) for women.[1] More recent books have considered what these changes and continuities have meant for different groups of women, and the relevance of gender within this, particularly from the Russian perspective.[2] One notable collection analysing transitional change and gender politics in Central and Eastern Europe is that by Tanya Renne,[3] which allows various individuals and very varied groups of women in Central and Eastern Europe to voice their experiences and perspectives on the social and political changes facing them.

The present collection of articles reviews elements of the decade of changes from the perspectives of gender and identity. Some contributions highlight feminist analyses and resistance to the negative consequences of certain changes for various groups in society and argue that women's activities have played a large part in securing democratic developments in various countries. Following from a gender-based analysis of formal public participation in politics in Slovenia through to an exploration of the shifting boundaries of gender and sexuality in youth cultural discourse in Russia, focus is on the importance of considerations of gender in thinking through change. Across the six articles is a common feminist definition of what is 'political'. That is, the authors do not view political participation in a narrow vein concerned only with functional aspects of the external, public world. The viewpoint that politics is about *relations of power* in society and how these are mediated can be clearly followed throughout. From the power of violence, to the power of ideas concerning motherhood, and to sexuality as a lever of power, it is clear that key sites of struggle are being analysed.

In each contribution the recognition that various identities are constructed at particular times and in certain conditions is apparent in assessing the particular locations of various women and women's groups and how these have changed and are changing through transitional times. Hilary Pilkington has pointed out in considering social identity that 'identities of gender, generation, sexuality, class, race, ethnicity and religion are constructed in time and space'.[4] Spanning a variety of constructions of gender and considering the ways in which these have been differently negotiated over time are key themes of the studies collected here. The term 'difference' is itself a key term in feminist analysis, and a mere tolerance of difference, as Audre Lorde long ago pointed out, is grossly reformist, since 'Difference must not be merely tolerated, but seen as a fund of necessary polarities between which our creativity can spark like a dialectic. Only then does the necessity for interdependency become unthreatening.'[5] Here Lorde is reiterating the basic humanist and feminist principle regarding the necessity to overcome fear and learned behaviour regarding differences as causes for separation and suspicion rather than as forces for change. In the various studies collected here, we see outlines of some women's abilities and willingess to overcome the fear of difference, recognize its existence in a multiplicity of areas, and use that knowledge to learn how to identify themselves and their goals, define their own terms and make common cause with others who share those visions.

Whether the authors are explicitly considering differences of, say, ethnicity as in the Bulgarian study, or of constructions of sexuality in the Russian article, the need for considering women's *experience* of change is crucial. The recognition that women's experiences are mediated by various constructions of how women should be, or what 'proper' women are, is highlighted in considerations of Soviet-type ideologies of womanhood as they clash with the recent realties of women's everyday lives and activities. That many women are actively involved in democratic projects within their countries and are linking with international networks and organizations highlights their key social and political *agency* in engendering change.

The spread of these articles falls into two loose groups across a continuum from more public and formal arenas of gender politics to more informal considerations of 'personal' aspects of gender discourses of sexuality. Recognition of women as both subjects and objects of change, with vast differentiation across and among groups of women, becomes apparent. At the outset Milica Antić considers the influences of Slovene political parties on the electoral politics of women, recognizing that such parties at first did not think of women as political agents. The striking discrepancy between promises regarding equal opportunities and their fulfilment was such that women began organizing themselves to draw the authorities' attention to the special and unenviable status of women. A turning-point emerges when women begin to use party organization and make use of the insitutions of the political system in order to change the status of women. It is notable that following each election (between 1990 and 1996) the gender structure changed significantly. While quotas for women as potential candidates and on key committees have been successful in many Western European countries, particularly those in Scandinavia, considerations of quota mechanisms in Slovenia are often perceived as a means of oppression of women, establishing inequality by placing the sexes in unequal positions. Antić concludes her analysis with a recognition that for quotas to be effective in gender parity then the political atmosphere must be favourably inclined towards the equality of men and women in the parties and within society as a whole.

In moving from this gender-based analysis of the possibilities for change in electoral politics, Delina Fico explores the development of women's organizations in Albania since 1990. The processes of formation and strengthening of the women's movement in Albania are assessed within considerations of the deep political and social changes that have been taking place – and are continuing – in the country following the collapse of the former regime. Fico shows how the processes of developing alliances emerged within women's politics, overcoming the divisions, real and imaginary, which had been in place in the strictly controlled social and political climate for 45 years. Again it is clear that the particular needs of women were largely overlooked by policy-makers, as is apparent elsewhere, and it was the self-organization of women themselves through Albanian women's NGOs that addressed women's social, legal and health issues in both rural and urban areas. The continuities and discontinuities from the previous era are made apparent in this consideration of political alliances within various sectors of civil society in tackling a series of obstacles ranging from the low awareness of women's rights to the lack of government recognition for the activities and importance of women's groups within society. It has often been foreign pressure which has pushed government authorities in the direction of giving women's NGOs the recognition they deserve. Women's personal commitments to engendering change in transforming Albanian society and in building democracy are clearly demonstrated in this survey.

Concentrating on research concerning issues of violence against women in Poland, Urszula Nowakowska pursues a focus on research and activities within the Women's Rights Centre and its interaction with state forces. The study is undertaken within an international frame of women's human rights and freedom from violence. Nowakowska measures the Polish reality against international standards and argues that, despite other major social changes in Poland, violence against women is still not recognized as a serious social problem, but remains hidden and marked by strong traditions of guilt and shame. Again consideration is given to how the development and establishment of women's autonomous groups can actively intervene in the processes of change within Polish society. Links are clear between the feminist groups and organizations across the international spectrum of activity towards ending the oppression of women through male violence in the home, on the streets, in prostitution and trafficking of women, through racial violence and internationally in war. The ways in which political changes in Poland have forced forward and backward swings in terms of openness to gender sensitivity are made clear with the new Minister for Family Affairs refusing to recognize the existence of the problem of violence against women. Public awareness campaigns about domestic violence are criticized as being aimed against the family and 'irrelevant'. Traditional myths about 'kind husbands' are hard to deconstruct and have political impact when previously agreed national Plans of Action, such as that for the Advancement of Women, are not enforced. The concluding plea for women's human rights is clearly a challenge to action.

This recognition of the strength of women's activities in contributing towards engendering change is considered from a different perspective in connection with women's actions to resist violence and authoritarian policies across those countries involved in the Yugoslav wars. This analysis considers the redefinition of some key concepts such as citizenship that is occurring in thinking through the civic resistance undertaken by some women's groups and non-governmental organizations (NGOs). In emphasizing aspects of women's civic engagements the author aims to unite theoretical explorations and practical engagements concerning women exercising and extending their citizenship and human rights.

In her consideration of the construction of Bulgarian women's self-identity over the past five decades, Tatyana Kotzeva considers the conflicting images of women constructed through Marxist frameworks and juxtaposes this with analyses from interviews with women in Bulgaria during 1997. In this way, the article raises questions about how both the images of 'socialist Amazon' and of 'women as mother' legitimate women's consciousness and behaviour. The ways in which women from three ethnic groups articulate different views on their security and the future are analysed and conclusions are raised regarding self-identification strategies. Although women approve of gender equality and emancipation at an abstract level, in their everyday lives the women interviewed tend to define themselves in relation to others and identify themselves with mothering and caring within the family. Kotzeva argues that, with the radical changes going on within society and the apparent barriers against women's access to public influence, it could be that the family becomes the only alternative arena in which women can invest their personal energies.

The final article continues this analytical mode regarding the construction of identities and self-images across the shifting boundaries of gender and sexuality. Elena Omel'chenko explores the construction of gender and sexuality in Russian youth culture through a study of three new Russian youth magazines. The reading of these magazines highlights the current shifts in the understanding of gender differences at the end of the 1990s. Within the fragmentation of the search for sexual identities in the particular post-Soviet moral climate, the dominant role of the media in the formation of sexual discourses is apparent. Both the siting of new sexual experience and the targets of sexual discourse are considered within the context of how sexual 'others' are portrayed. The means of 'othering' can be undertaken within a context of what is normal and what is abnormal, and as such could create hierarchies of difference. In concluding that sexuality is a key lever of power in contemporary Russian society it is apparent that it is also a key site of struggle for the youth audience. While Russian youth magazines work at a similar level to those in the West, Omel'chenko points out that, unlike Western discourse, non-traditional sexualities are employed in Russian youth magazines as a challenge to the youth audience. These challenges are presented in ways which link sexuality to wider philosophical and ideological questions within Russian society.

The recognition that 'the personal is political' is apparent throughout this collection. In her words, Delina Fico argues that the building of the women's movement in Albania 'was our way of transforming ourselves, learning democracy, building democracy in our own territory, and building the movement and the experience of working within it'. The cultural symbol *Woman* has long been recognized as one which political movements make use of within nationalist discourse and in terms of political power struggles at various levels. This collection highlights women as agents of change, as active participants in various movements for democracy and in opposition to violence and oppression. However, as is noted by several authors, social differentiation is such that some women's gains can be others' losses and the complex fabric of post-Soviet societies is such that general perspectives cannot be sustained. The intellectual task of scholars engaged in analyses of complex social change is enhanced by studies which consider the intersections of issues of ethnicity, class, gender, sexuality, religion and so on. The participation of all members of society on an equal footing is viewed as a basic human right, and it seems that over the past decade women's involvement in many arenas of change in Central and Eastern

European countries has been something which is only now being fully recognized.

NOTES

1. See, for example, Chris Corrin (ed.), *Superwomen and the Double Burden: Women's Experience of Change in Central and Eastern Europe and the Former Soviet Union* (London: Scarlet, 1992); Barbara Einhorn, *Cinderella Goes to Market: Citizenship, Gender, and Women's Movements in East Central Europe* (London: Verso, 1993); Nanette Funk and Marcia Mueller (eds.), *Gender Politics and Post-Communism: Reflections from Eastern Europe and the Former Soviet Union* (London: Routledge, 1993); Shirin Rai, Hilary Pilkington and Annie Phizacklea (eds.), *Women in the Face of Change: The Soviet Union, Eastern Europe and China* (London: Routledge, 1992); Marilyn Rueschmeyer (ed.), *Women in the Politics of Postcommunist Eastern Europe* (Armonk, NY and London: M.E. Sharpe, 1994).
2. Sue Bridger, Rebecca Kay and Kathryn Pinnick, *No More Heroines: Russia, Women and the Market* (London: Routledge, 1996); Mary Buckley (ed.), *Post-Soviet Women: From the Baltic to Central Asia* (Cambridge: Cambridge University Press, 1997); Rosalind Marsh (ed.), *Women in Russia and Ukraine* (Cambridge: Cambridge University Press, 1996); Hilary Pilkington (ed.), *Gender, Generation and Identity in Contemporary Russia* (London: Routledge, 1996); Anastasia Posadskaya (ed.), *Women in Russia: A New Era in Russian Feminism* (London: Verso, 1994).
3. Tanya Renne (ed.), *Ana's Land: Sisterhood in Eastern Europe* (Boulder, CO and Oxford: Westview, 1997).
4. Pilkington (ed.), *Gender, Generation and Identity in Contemporary Russia*, p.1.
5. Audre Lorde, quotation from 1979, reprinted in *The Audre Lorde Compendium* (London: The Women's Press, 1996), p.159.

Slovene Political Parties and Their Influence on the Electoral Prospects of Women

MILICA ANTIĆ GABER

An exploration of the theories of equal participation of men and women within the new parties in Slovenian political life alongside the realities of gender parity allows questions to be raised concerning the gendered nature of citizenship within the new political climate in Slovenia. It is apparent that the gender balance changed in the elections between 1990 and 1996. The development of women's groups and forums, first outside the political party structures and later within them, highlights the ways in which women's self-organization used governmental mechanisms to challenge inequities of Slovenian party political life. The efforts and the range of activities undertaken by women's groups draw attention to the provisions which need to be made if the parties are to make transparent their policy towards the issue of 'equal presence'. Most parties confine themselves to the verbal strategies of supporting women's entry into politics and are unwilling to take steps or adopt strategies involving positive action, such as quotas. The result of such a policy in Slovenia (definitely not only due to the parties) is that there are only seven women among 90 deputies in lower house of parliament. It is recognized that, even if quotas were implemented, these alone would not be sufficient because what is needed is a political atmosphere that is favourably disposed towards the equality of men and women within political parties and in society as a whole.

Slovenia is a relatively small Central–Eastern European state established in 1991. It was the most developed and the most westernized part of Yugoslavia before the downfall of the federal socialist state. Geographically it is situated east of Italy, south of Austria and north of Croatia. It is a member of the Council of Europe, and is in the process of integration into the European Union and NATO.

After the fall of the Berlin wall, Slovenia saw the formation of political parties of classic representative democracy. It is true that not all called themselves parties, yet that is what they were. The highlight of 1990 was the first democratic and multiparty election, in which 20 parties' lists of candidates and some independent candidates took part. The most prosperous were: the Party of Democratic Renewal (now the United List of Social Democrats – ULSD), the Liberal Democratic Party (now Liberal Democracy of Slovenia – LDS), Slovenian Christian Democrats – SCD, the Slovenian Farmers' Party (now Slovenian People's Party – SPP), the Slovenian Democratic Alliance – SDA, the Democratic Party (a part of the

SDA), Greens of Slovenia – GS, the Social Democratic Party of Slovenia (now the Social Democratic Party – SDP), the Socialist Alliance of Slovenia – SAS, the Liberal Party – LP, and the Slovenian National Party – SNP. Some of the parties were transformed socio-political organizations (such as the Communist Party or the Alliance of Socialist Youth), some of them arose from oppositional movements, and some were organized from new social movements (such as the Greens and the peace movement). Nine parties won seats in the first multiparty, three-chamber assembly.

The political interests of women within the processes of transition were duly recognized as legitimate interests of one social group, yet realization of those interests did not receive appropriate attention: 'Big issues' were in the forefront instead. The issue of establishing a sovereign country for the Slovene nation was a laarge task that subsumed all others, including the issue of the social status of women. It appears that, at least for a limited time, there prevailed the belief that women's right to vote made them legally and politically equal to men, while it was a question of free choice of any individual how she or he would choose to make use of this right. This belief exaggerates the importance of formal equality of women and neglects the importance of social inequalities which decisively influence political inequality.[1]

Feminist circles have often posed the question of whether a democracy that disregards the political equality of women is a democracy at all in the true sense of the word. Some refer to such a democracy as 'unfinished democracy' while more radical feminists use the term 'male democracy'.[2] At that time, the new political organizations (parties) in Slovenia did not initially think of women as political agents. Women were perceived as a relatively significant part of the electorate whose support had to be enlisted at certain decisive moments, particularly at election time. With the exception of the former Alliance of Socialist Youth – which at its 1989 congress espoused the demand for the establishment of a 'Ministry for Women', followed a year later by the inclusion in its programme of a chapter entitled 'For a Policy of Equal Opportunities' – party programmes did not devote much attention to so-called women's issues. These programmes provide evidence that no parties tackled the issue of women seriously and thoroughly. What came to the foreground were 'strategic issues': the economic survival of the nation, the nation's individuality, the establishment of statehood and the issue of the Slovene army.

Some parties kept promising equal participation in lists of candidates – that is, equal opportunities for political action – but there was a striking discrepancy between promises and their fulfilment. It seems that this was yet another reason why women took the task of organizing themselves into their own hands. A number of independent women's groups emerged, trying in different ways to draw the authorities' attention to the special and unenviable status of women.

How Do Party Statutes and Programmes Deal with the Equality of Women?

Party programmes and statutes are the main party documents in which the parties' relationship within particular area of political activity can be observed. Apart from the Social Democratic Party of Slovenia, all the above-mentioned parties have enshrined provisions concerning the equality of women into their programme objectives and principles. The Slovene People's Party perceives women as 'an agent on an equal footing with men in all spheres of social life', while the realization of their equal status depends on economic prosperity and the standard of living, and in the party's opinion the position is unsatisfactory. Among the programme objectives of the United List of Social Democrats dealing with these issues, pride of place is given to the achievement of social equality for both men and women, freedom, solidarity between men and women, and partnership. The Liberal Democracy of Slovenia underlines the duty of the state to make it possible for women to pass from the private to the public and political sphere and vice versa to the same extent as men, as well as to have equal opportunities within these spheres. By their success in the initiative whereby women would be able to choose prolonged maternity leave, the Slovene Christian Democrats aim at 'equating the opportunities for women to have a professional career with those of their male colleagues'. Also in line with the Christian Democratic ideology is their demand for a moral and material evaluation of motherhood and fatherhood.

As far as women's participation in politics and party demands to this effect are concerned, it is notable that only three parties have enshrined these demands in their documents. The programme objectives of the Slovene People's Party include the creation of 'conditions for equal participation of women in politics and social life'. The United List of Social Democrats gives further substance to its demand: it espouses parity democracy, perceived as democracy 'in which political participation by both sexes is put on an equal footing, meaning systematically training and encouraging women to take part in politics'. The Liberal Democracy of Slovenia notes that it is in favour of 'the enforcement of quotas as one of the mechanisms to ensure the participation of both male and female representatives of social minorities in parliament as well as in governing and other political bodies'. One may fairly rapidly conclude that there is some discrepancy between publicly declared views and the actual state of affairs, particularly regarding the proportion of women in important party bodies, the party leadership and the parliamentary party groups (see Table 1).[3]

TABLE 1

WOMEN IN POLITICAL PARTIES

Party	Year	Percentage of Party Women Members	Percentage of Women in Party Bodies	Women in Party Leadership	Percentage of Women in Parliamentary Group
SPP	1993	33.3	22.7 (Executive Committee)		20.0
	1997	35.0	18.4 (Executive Committee)	1 Vice President out of 5	5.2
SDPS	1993	20.3	10.5 (Presidency)	***	0
	1996	28.0	***	***	6.3
ULSD	1993	37.3	17.5 (Presidency) 16.7 (Party Council)	1 Vice President out of 3	14.3
	1997	35.6	18.3 (Presidency) 16.7 (Party Council)	1 Vice President out of 3	0
LDS	1993	28.3	27.2 (Executive Committee) 26.6 (Party Council)	1 Vice President out of 3	9.1
	1997	30.1	27.2 (Executive Committee) 27.0 (Party Council)	1 Vice President out of 3	4.0
SNP	1993	18.0	12.0 (Presidency)	***	8.3
	1997	***	***	***	33.3
SCD	1993	61.7	18.6 (Presidency)	1 Vice President	20.0
	1997	60.0	23.0 (Executive Committee)	1 Secretary General	10.0
DPPS[a]	1997	31.0	13.3 (Presidency)		20.0

[a] DPPS = Democratic Party of Pensioners of Slovenia   *** Information not available

The largest discrepancy in terms of the percentage of women party members and their representation in party leadership and other party bodies may be observed among the Slovene Christian Democrats, who have the largest overall percentage of women party members. Following the 1996 parliamentary election, the largest discrepancy between the percentage of women party members and their percentage in the parliamentary group may be observed in the United List of Social Democrats. The proportion is in balance in neither party; the smallest discrepancy may be observed in the Democratic Party of Pensioners of Slovenia (DPPS).

Women's Sections in the Parties

The shift from special non-party women's organizations to the party organization of women may also be viewed in the context of the restructuring of the Slovene political arena. As in most European countries, women in Slovenia realized that it was the parties that controlled the political arena and that they could continue to reshape this arena only if they organized themselves within the parties, thereby achieving greater influence. They began to put into effect the assertion that women should occupy the highest party posts, and the idea that it was necessary to break through the barrier represented by the election machine became widely accepted: women's previous negative view of official – party and national – politics changed. Making use of the institutions of the political system in order to change the status of women became the new motto of women's party activities.

On this basis, women's alliances, clubs and forums were established. They include the following:

- the Women's Forum, created from the Women's faction of the Party of Democratic Renewal (the present ULSD);

- the Slovene Women's Alliance within the Slovene Christian Democrats;

- the Women's Alliance within the Slovene People's Party;

- the Committee of Social Democrats within the Social Democratic Party of Slovenia;

- the Minerva Club and the Women's Network within the Liberal Democracy of Slovenia.

The Women's Forum sees its role in providing possibilities for the ULSD 'to formulate a principled policy of equal opportunities for both sexes, help strengthen the political stature of women within the party itself and enable civil society groups striving to achieve similar goals to exert a direct influence on the United List and on Parliament'.

The Slovene Women's Alliance unites women from all social backgrounds upholding the Slovene Christian Democrats' programme and wishing to contribute to formulating a policy based on the principles of Christian democracy. The following, *inter alia*, have been included among its tasks and aims: it 'represents political and organizational interests and demands in all the bodies of the SCD; ... participates in forming public opinion and in decision-making both in the public and within the SCD, particularly in drawing up lists of candidates and their selection. In doing so, it strives to achieve balanced representation of both female and male candidates; ... gives their women members, functionaries and alliance mandate holders political instruction and training ... .'

The wide spectrum of programme provisions of the Women's Alliance within the Slovene People's Party draws attention to the fact that their activity focuses on the society as a whole and not on the party. They advocate, among other things, 'the enforcement of the already acquired women's rights in politics and society; the development and enforcement of possibilities for the inclusion of women in political and social life; the inclusion of women in politics at a local, municipal and national level' and so forth.

As far as women's participation in politics is concerned, it was the Liberal Democracy of Slovenia which first put it into practice by introducing quotas for lists of candidates competing for elected party bodies[4] and later for parliamentary elections as well. During the run-up to the 1996 election, the United List of Social Democrats, too, at its November 1995 Slovenj Gradec congress included in its statutes a provision to set quotas.[5] In other parties women did not put forward such or similar demands; they were of the opinion that women should compete for parliamentary seats on an equal footing with their male colleagues. The need to adopt measures of positive discrimination has hitherto received relatively little attention in Slovenia.

The Role of Parties in the Candidate Selection Procedure

A party is a political actor vying for power, for the largest possible number of parliamentary seats, thereby being given the opportunity to implement its political programme. In the countries with a long-standing democratic election tradition, in which the political system is not subject to fundamental change, the parties know exactly what to do (whom to put forward as a candidate and where) in order to achieve the desired result. From this point of view, the situation in Slovenia is still relatively unstable. However, following three elections and with fundamentally unaltered legislation, certain indicators may already be identified regarding the support of certain parties in individual electoral units (constituencies) and even in electoral districts.

In some countries, the law provides for a precisely defined method of selecting candidates for parliamentary elections. In Slovenia, the law stipulates only that lists of candidates shall be determined by parties in a secret ballot in accordance with their internal rules.[6] The law stipulates neither the method of selection of candidates by the parties nor the method of drawing up their lists of candidates and the principles on the basis of which certain candidates are favoured rather than others. Who in fact makes these decisions?

In the year preceding an election, parties commission various opinion polls and predictions of the prospects of would-be candidates, as well as following the opinion polls on party popularity published by the mass media. However, the electoral headquarters of individual parties usually operate in strict secrecy and only a very select few can influence the adoption of final decisions. The first circle whose candidacies are handled by the party consist of the most high-profile party individuals: MPs, ministers, state secretaries, mayors and individuals from the highest echelons of the party apparatus. These are mostly men.

The second circle is drawn from the candidates from regional and local centres. They are identified by party committees from their own members or from party sympathizers and consist of prominent local individuals (including above all doctors, company directors, lawyers and school headmasters). The committees' task is to persuade these candidates to stand as candidates on the party's list. Since there are few women in the highest managerial positions, women are poorly represented as candidates in this circle.

The third circle is to some extent special to the case of Slovenia. In countries with long tradition of democratic elections, a selection procedure is carried out whereby individuals – male and female – with a long record of party activity who consider themselves qualified to stand report to the party and officials from the party apparatus interview them and prepare them for candidacy. In Slovenia, by contrast, the procedure of identifying candidates is carried out in precisely the opposite manner: the party leadership searches for well-known, renowned and high-profile individuals with a positive 'image' likely to attract voters. This may be demonstrated by the presence of numerous 'well-known faces' from cultural circles, the media and some important state institutions, whom the electorate had never before associated with the party. Membership of a party, therefore, does not pose a significant obstacle, nor indeed is it an advantage, as far as standing for a seat in parliament is concerned. In this category, women are present alongside other well-known public figures from cultural circles and the media.

The fourth circle consists of members in local committees with many years' service to the party, who – either in their own opinion or in that of the local committees – could make a good party candidate in elections. This circle is the largest one and the chances of standing as a candidate from within it are equally poor for candidates of both sexes.

So far, only one party in Slovenia, the United List of Social Democrats, has made the selection of candidates transparent. The ULSD selected its candidates by internal election, thereby demonstrating a markedly democratic organizational structure on the part of that party.

After a review of statutory provisions of the major parliamentary parties regarding the procedures for candidate selection, the following basic conclusions may be drawn:

1. The most democratic procedure for drawing up and approving lists of candidates has been established by the ULSD and the Democratic Party (DP).

2. As a rule, in all the parties, lists of candidates are determined or

approved (or both) by the principal bodies of the party. In these, as demonstrated in Table 2, women are poorly represented and have no real power. This is one of the main reasons for their failure to be included in their parties' lists of candidates for parliamentary elections in any significant numbers. It is surprising, though, that even in those parties in which they represent a large portion of the membership and in which women's alliances or factions exist, these play no role in the candidate-selection procedure.

TABLE 2

PERCENTAGES OF WOMEN IN LISTS OF CANDIDATES AND PARTY PARLIAMENTARY GROUPS

| | Candidates | | | | Members of Parliament | | | |
| | 1992 election | | 1996 election | | 1992 election | | 1996 election | |
	number	per cent	number	per cent	number	per cent	number	per cent
LDS	7	9.3	11	13.6	2	9.09	1	4.0
SCD	10	11.2	8	9.52	2	13.3	1	10.0
ULSD	14	15.5	36	40.9	2	14.2	0	0
SNP	4	7.0	6	10.7	2	16.6	1	25.0
SPP	7	8.7	11	13.6	2	20.0	1	5.2
DP	12	13.9	20	24.4	1	16.6	0	0
UL	12	14.9	12	23.1	0	0	0	0
SDPS	6	7.9	10	11.9	0	0	1	6.2
DPPS			17	21.8			1	20.0

In considering the reasons for the small percentage of women appearing in lists of candidates, it remains indisputable that there is a striking discrepancy between this percentage and the proportion of women in the population of the country. In lists of candidates for all the elections so far, women have had a 14- to 19-per-cent share. Even at first glance, this striking discrepancy is evident, while a more detailed picture is provided by the electoral bias, calculated by dividing the share of women in the electorate with the share of women candidates: for the 1992[7] election this amounted to 3.5, and for the 1996[8] election to 2.7.

The percentage of women in lists of candidates is not satisfactory either if compared with the total percentage of women members of Slovene parties.[9] Table 3 shows that the percentage of women members in Slovene parties is much higher than the percentage of women in lists of candidates for parliamentary elections and in their parties' parliamentary groups in the National Assembly (NA).[10]

TABLE 3

PERCENTAGE OF WOMEN IN PARLIAMENTARY PARTY MEMBERSHIP, IN LISTS
OF CANDIDATES AND IN THE NATIONAL ASSEMBLY

	Percentage of Women in the Party		Percentage of Women in Lists of Candidates		Percentage of Women in the National Assembly	
	1992	1996	1992	1996	1992	1996
LDS	28.3	30.2	9.3	13.6	9.9	4.0
SCD	61.7	60.0	11.2	9.5	13.3	10.0
ULSD	37.3	35.6	15.5	40.9	14.2	–
SNP	18.0	–	7.0	8.9	16.6	25.0
SDP	20.3	28.0[a]	7.9	11.9	1.0	6.2
SPP	33.3	35.0	8.7	13.6	20.0	5.2

Note: [a] The percentage of women in the Social Democratic Party for 1996 is based on an individual assessment. It was published in the daily *Dnevnik* on 20 December 1996 (author Borut Mehle).

On the basis of lists of candidates of all the parties submitted for the 1992 parliamentary elections one may draw the conclusion that most women candidates were entered by the parties least likely to be represented in parliament. The largest proportion of female candidates could be observed in the small non-parliamentary parties: the Christian Socialist list (30 per cent), followed by the Slovene Ecological Movement (26.9 per cent) and the Independent Party (20 per cent).

In lists of candidates of those parties that were most likely to be represented in parliament there were significantly fewer women candidates. The United List had the largest proportion (15.5 per cent), followed by the Greens of Slovenia (14.9 per cent), the Democratic Party (13.9 per cent), the Slovene Christian Democrats (11.2 per cent) and the Liberal Democrats (9.3 per cent).

In terms of percentages of women, there were no significant changes in candidate lists for the 1996 parliamentary election (with the exception of the ULSD lists). All parties, with the exception of the SCD, increased slightly the percentage of women in lists of candidates – perhaps a trifling increase but nevertheless an increase. Out of 1,311 candidates, there were 246 women (19 per cent). Compared to the previous election, with 1,475 candidates and only 219 women (14.8 per cent), the share of women increased by almost five percentage points. The most significant increase in the share of women could be seen in the ULSD lists. A new party, the Democratic Party of Pensioners of Slovenia (DPPS), entered parliament; its proportion of women candidates totalled 21.8 per cent. In these elections, too, it was parties unlikely to be represented in parliament that had a high proportion of women. A higher percentage than the average was noted in some small non-parliamentary parties: the lists of candidates of both 'green' parties (23.1 and 29.1 per cent), of the Party of Equal Provinces (45 per cent), of the Republican Alliance of Slovenia (35.3 per cent) and of the Christian Social Union (28 per cent).

Following each election, the gender structure has changed significantly. To the 90 parliamentary seats in the Slovene National Assembly, 78 men and 12 women (13.3 per cent) were elected in the 1992 election. Two women members of the Liberal Democracy of Slovenia, the party that had the largest share of the vote, took their seats in the National Assembly, as did two Christian Democrats as the second party and the ULSD as the third party, alongside two women members of the Slovene National Party and of the Slovene People's Party. One female MP came from the Democratic Party (DP), while the Greens of Slovenia and the Social Democratic Party had none. Through members' changing party allegiance, individual MPs' assuming posts in the government or returning to the National Assembly from the government, and some leaving the National Assembly, the percentage of women members of party parliamentary groups changed slightly, which nevertheless did not significantly affect the proportion of women in the National Assembly.

In 1996 seven women took their seats in the National Assembly, meaning that, compared with the share of women MPs in the preceding parliament, their share dropped by 6.5 percentage points and amounted to 7.8 per cent. Except for the ULSD which has no woman MP, all other parliamentary groups have one woman MP each, and one woman MP represents the Hungarian ethnic community.

In the 1992 election, the largest discrepancy between the share of female candidates and the share of elected women MPs may be noted in the Greens of Slovenia, while the smallest may be noted in the case of all three largest parliamentary parties. In the 1996 election the most surprising discrepancy may be noted in the proportion of candidates and those elected in the ULSD, where out of 36 female candidates none received a sufficient number of votes. At the same time, it has to be said that the low percentages of women per party are fairly evenly distributed. Following the 1992 election, regardless of the parties' differing attitudes to women's participation and support in politics, they had in most cases two women MPs and, following the 1996 election, only one woman MP. The relationship between the share of female candidates and elected MPs is shown in Table 2, which presents data on election day.

Table 4 demonstrates that, in the 1990 and 1992 elections, there was no significant discrepancy between the share of female candidates and the number of elected female MPs, which may be accounted for by the possibilities provided by the system of proportional representation. Above all, this holds true of 1990 elections to the social–political chamber, when parties in their electoral districts submitted lists of candidates, while individual party candidates collected votes in the electoral district and not in the electoral unit. The unit in which voting took place and from which the candidate was elected was therefore the same.

In considering the results of the 1990 and 1992 elections, account should be taken of the fact that some female candidates took their seats in the National Assembly thanks to the division of the remaining votes, which were distributed among parties from the national lists, while in the most recent election the national list for the division of mandates based on the remaining votes existed solely in the Christian Democratic Party – and in no other parliamentary party – from which no woman MP was elected.

TABLE 4

FEMALE CANDIDATES AND ELECTED WOMEN MPS IN MULTIPARTY
ELECTIONS HELD TO DATE (PERCENTAGES)

	1990 election SPC	1992 election NA	1996 election NA
Female candidates	17.9	14.8	19.0
Women MPs elected	15.0	13.3	7.8

Alongside the reasons for election failure in 1996, which derive from the characteristics of the electoral system, one must not forget the role of the parties themselves.

First, it is obvious that in the 1996 election – in general, and especially as far as women were concerned – 'election geometry' played its role: it seems that parties had learnt a great deal in the process of proceeding from one election to the next. Parliamentary elections were conducted for a second time on the basis of same system; local elections took place in the intervening period, which allowed party leaderships to come to conclusions about the electoral units and electoral districts in which their party had the best prospects, those in which it was likely to collect a significant portion of the vote, and those in which it was likely to do worse. Naturally, the 'party men' (eloquently nicknamed 'gatekeepers' in some parts, whereas in Slovenia they are called 'election headquarters') kept this information to themselves. The more aggressive, more combative or more calculating candidates, with greater political power and influence, were thus able to retain 'winnable' electoral units – those in which they deemed voters would certainly vote for 'their party', irrespective of who stood as a candidate.

Second, empirical research shows that shifts in the electorate in terms of favouring a certain party are also reflected in the election of women. The rule is fairly simple: when a party is winning votes, the proportion of elected women usually increases, and when a party is losing votes, this share decreases. According to Darcy's calculations, winning and losing votes may account for 62 per cent of the variance in women's success in winning and losing votes. A significant shift in winning votes – regardless of whether this is occurring on the left or on the right – should bring to the party an increase in the share of women elected as well.

If one tests this formula in the Slovene case and adds to it the shift from one ideological sphere to the other, one discerns that in the 1996 election the SPP, SDP and SCD party grouping, which in ideological terms may be placed to the right of centre, won votes in numbers exceeding those of the 1992 election by 18.59 percentage points, whereas the loss of the voters' support by the left party grouping (LDS, ULSD, DP) amounted to six percentage points, which could to a large extent explain the significant reduction of female representation in the National Assembly. The percentage of women in those parties which did well did not increase in any significant way. In fact, their percentage dropped significantly, which may also have resulted from the fact that only seven women candidates from the above-mentioned parties from the centre-right were competing in 'winnable' electoral units and as many as 21 were competing in the 'lost' electoral units. The percentage of women in the parties which gained almost 19 percentage points – that is, 16 MPs – dropped from 13.8 per cent in the 1992 election to 6.7 per cent four years later. The share of women in parties whose result was reduced by six percentage points was also reduced from 11.8 per cent in 1992 to 8.8 per cent in 1996.

Third, one of the reasons for the disappointing overall result achieved by women in elections is also the shift of the electorate in the direction of traditionalism.[11] The fundamental shifts in the electorate regarding individual parties which exerted an influence on the (non-)election of women include an increase in the share of votes for the Social Democratic Party, which in the 1992 election almost failed to cross the threshold for entry into parliament (whereas in the following election it collected 16.13 per cent of the vote), and a significant increase in the number of votes cast for the Slovene People's Party, whose 19.38 per cent of the vote in the last election made it the second largest party (previously it attained 8.75 per cent).

Political analyses elsewhere in the world highlight the fact that large 'shifts' on the part of the electorate itself usually have an influence on the decrease in the proportion of women elected from the parties which are losing votes. This rule regarding negative influences is further substantiated if the shift is towards parties upholding traditional values, which also manifest their orientation by the proportion of women in their lists of candidates. To this should be added the fact that two parties of what by European standards represents the centre – the Democrats of Slovenia (DS) (with 24.4 per cent of women in their lists) and the green parties (the Greens of Slovenia with 23.1 per cent, and the Green Alternative with 29.1 per cent) failed to secure election to parliament after the split. There is no woman MP who in the past two years would reach the upper third of the percentages expressed in popularity polls. If one adds the defeat of the party of the left, which was the only one to legislate for female quotas within the party, but whose election result decreased by 4.5 percentage points, the failure of women in this election may be adequately explained, at least in statistical terms.[12]

Repeat Candidacies (Incumbency)

In elections – particularly in the first-past-the-post electoral systems, where each candidate stands in his or her own electoral unit – those who are already MPs or in the government have a distinct advantage. They have a good chance of being elected unless the party is broadly losing the support of the electorate. In other electoral systems also, members of parliament, whether male or female, have the advantage of being known to the public, thereby increasing their chances of being elected. This is precisely why parties favour such candidacies. In some countries, the share of those who repeatedly stand as candidates and are re-elected amounts to more than 90 per cent.[13]

The fact that during the National Assembly's preceding term women constituted only 13 per cent of MPs, allied to the above-mentioned high rate of re-election, provides yet another explanation of why women's chances of being elected are so small. In Slovenia also, a significant number of MPs, male and female alike, stood again as candidates. Out of 90 MPs, 70 stood again as candidates (77.8 per cent): of 77 male MPs, 59 or 76.6 per cent stood again as candidates; of 13 women MPs, 11 or 84.6 per cent stood again. Of all those standing again as candidates, 30 members (42.8 per cent) were re-elected, comprising 28 male and 2 female MPs; 30 of the male MPs were re-elected (50.8 per cent) and 2 females (18.2 per cent).[14] The data show that there were 2.5 times as many re-elections of male MPs as of females.

In order to clarify this state of affairs, it should also be borne in mind that, in addition to the influence exerted on the election in Slovenia by the electoral units, present and former ministers and mayors also stood as candidates on various lists, and these had no difficulty in being allowed to take part in the election campaign. The parliamentary party candidacies included 14 male and two female ministers, and five of the male ministers being elected; however, no minister from either of the governing parties of the former coalition, the ULSD and the SCD, was elected; these two parties' election results were significantly poorer. Out of five elected ministers, four were LDS candidates and one was a candidate of the SDP.

In fact, all the parties with mayors among their members staked their hopes on them, and it is becoming increasingly clear that they were not mistaken. Of the candidates put forward, there were 41 mayors, mostly in the LDS, SPP and SDP with ten mayors each, in the SCD with seven mayors and four in the ULSD. Out of 41 candidates, 25 were elected – six from the LDS lists, eight from the SPP lists, two from the SCD lists, and three from the ULSD lists. Their electability was therefore extremely high – the proportion of those elected amounted to 60.9 per cent.

After taking account of all the well-known party 'luminaries' (MPs, ministers, mayors) who took as many as 60 parliamentary seats (almost two-thirds), not much opportunity remained for the election of new candidates, including women.[15] The largest number of replacements of MPs occurred in the parliamentary group of the two parties that won most seats, the Slovene People's Party and the Social Democratic Party. Among these there were quite a few mayors of small municipalities who enjoyed the support of locals, and who were therefore not newcomers to the political arena.

Some Other Influences on the Presence of Women in the National Assembly

To the influences cited above could be added some others which contribute – although to a lesser extent – to the success or failure of women in a given election and which also contributed to the 1996 election in Slovenia. One such influence is the relationship between the number of votes cast in elections for a party and the number of female MPs elected.

As a rule, the party's size should exert a positive influence on women's chances of election. However, one can hardly state that the chances for the election of women are directly proportional to the number of votes cast for a party in elections. The only certainty is that the chances of women's election increase with the chances of the party winning additional votes. If a party estimates that it stands a greater chance in elections and if at the same time it estimates that it will win additional seats, it will be more favourably inclined towards women's candidacies than if it estimates that it is losing the support of the electorate. The 'green' parties are obviously an exception, since they include on average a larger number of female candidates on their lists and the share of women in their parliamentary groups is relatively high. However, these are parties which capture only about five per cent of the vote in elections.

In Slovenia, parties failed to conform to this tendency in the 1996 election. Parties which according to election forecasts were expecting relatively good results did not include a large number of women on their lists, especially not in 'electable' places. One may even draw the opposite conclusion: parties which it was clear in advance would be less successful in elections had a much better instinct for the placement of women on lists of candidates than those which preserved or increased electoral support. A deviation from the otherwise firm rule was also characteristic of the most powerful party, the LDS, which enjoys the support of more than a quarter of the electorate, and in whose lists of candidates and the parliamentary group may be observed a striking discrepancy between the presence of female MPs and both the percentage of women members of the party and its election results.

In an attempt to determine why, in the 1996 Slovene election, the above rule did not apply, one may look at two features. The first and obvious factor concerns the immaturity of the political arena in Slovenia as far as the issues of equality of the sexes and the like are concerned. The awareness of the importance, including the political importance, of the presence of women in party lists has not yet established itself either in the parties or in the electorate. The second factor (the two factors are complementary and contradictory at the same time) is provided by the powerful awareness of the likelihood of a close-run contest as far as the relationship between the so-called centre-left and centre-right party grouping was concerned. Any 'risk-taking with untried female candidates' was therefore construed as a major risk, as a 'gamble' which a party should not and could not indulge in at this political juncture (see Table 5).

The Importance of Policy on Quotas

One of the most important issues for the future of an evenly balanced representation of women in the National Assembly is the issue of quotas. Two important subdivisons of this issue concern the free establishment of quotas by the parties and the compulsory introduction of special women's quotas in the state law (an obligation for all the parties). Quotas are known as a mechanism whereby unprivileged or marginalized social groups, national minorities or other important social groups can be present in the lists of candidates for parliamentary elections. In the socialist period quotas were a means whereby the League of Communists enforced the principle of the presence of a certain share of some social groups in important political bodies. Significant social groups included women, the young, peasants and workers. However, the political bodies in which representatives of the above-mentioned groups were also present did not have any real power, and

TABLE 5

POLITICAL POWER OF THE PARTY AND PERCENTAGE OF WOMEN
IN THE PARLIAMENTARY GROUP

		National Assembly (votes)		National Assembly (seats)		Parliamentary Group (women MPs)	
		number	per cent	number	per cent	number	per cent
LDS	1992	278,638	23.4	22	24.4	2	9.9
	1996	288,783	27.1	25	27.8	1	4.0
SCD	1992	172,304	14.5	15	16.6	2	13.3
	1996	102,851	9.6	10	11.1	1	10.0
ULSD	1992	161,297	13.6	14	15.5	2	14.2
	1996	96,597	9.0	9	10.0	0	0
SNP	1992	119,010	10.2	12	13.3	2	16.6
	1996	34,422	3.2	4	4.4	1	25.0
SPP	1992	103,199	8.7	10	11.1	2	20.0
	1996	207,186	19.4	19	21.1	1	5.2
SDP	1992	395,650	3.3	4	4.4	0	0
	1996	172,470	16.3	16	17.8	1	6.2
DP	1992	59,460	5.0	6	6.6	1	16.6
	1996	28,624	2.7	0	0	0	0
UL	1992	44,002	3.7	5	5.5	0	0
	1996	–	–	–	–	–	–
DPPS	1992	–	–	–	–	–	–
	1996	46,152	4.3	5	5.6	1	20.0

for this reason this was a mechanism which failed to serve its primary purpose. It was bad experiences with the attempt to 'expand the potential' in socialism that led certain countries after the collapse of socialist regimes to reject quotas as an inappropriate means of ensuring the participation of women in politics.[16]

In Slovenia, too, similar views may be identified. In public the quota system is often perceived as a means of oppression, of the establishment of inequality, or of placing one of the sexes (the male sex) into an unequal position. Although discussions regarding quotas are not a complete novelty in Slovenia, quotas as a mechanism for a more appropriate level of representation of women in politics are still being rejected by the majority of the Slovene political parties.

As previously mentioned, discussions regarding quotas surfaced in 1989 in the predecessor of the LDS, the Alliance of Socialist Youth, as a programme provision in favour of target quotas. Three years later, this rather vague programme definition was further refined in the programme and the statutes of the LDS. In the programme part of the congress document, in the chapter entitled 'For a Policy of Equal Opportunities', the following definition is given:

The party shall implement the principle of equal representation of each sex within the organization, including the lists for elections to the assembly. In order gradually to attain the target of female representation (the representation of one of the sexes shall not deviate from the representation of the other sex by more than 5 to 10 per cent), the Liberal Democratic Party shall temporarily determine a minimum 30 per cent participation of each of the sexes in party bodies at least at the level of the state, and in its lists at least for elections into the National Assembly.

The party failed to live up to its programme goals in the 1992 election, however: only 9.3 per cent of candidates on its lists were women. Statutory provisions were brought closer to perfection by the party at its second congress in 1992, when the party took account of these provisions in elections to party bodies, which in turn exerted an influence on the increased representation of women in the Party Council (26.6 per cent) and in the Executive Committee (27.2 per cent). The statutes adopted by the party at its third congress in 1994 preserved the provision about a minimum one-third representation of each sex in the elected and appointed collegiate bodies of the party at the national level. Article 15 contains the following additional provision: 'In lists of candidates for election to the National Assembly submitted by the Executive Committee to the Party Council both sexes shall be represented on an equal footing.' However, the interpretation prevailed according to which the provision in question applied to the first selection of candidates only and not to the final list of candidates, which is approved by the Council and with which the party joins the election battle. This was why in the last election there were only 11 (13.6 per cent) female candidates in the LDS lists of candidates for the election to the National Assembly, substantially less than what is stipulated in the programme definition of the equal participation of both sexes and the target quotas of the party's predecessor at its 1989 congress.

Quotas were also adopted by the United List as a mechanism whereby a party could encourage greater opportunities for women in politics. As noted above, at its second congress in 1995 the party decided in favour of quotas within the party as well as quotas for elections to the National Assembly and municipal and local councils and for the election of mayors. The statutes contain the following provision regarding elected party bodies: 'Lists of candidates for the collegiate bodies of the party at all levels shall provide for a minimum 40 per cent representation of one sex unless this is prevented by the structure of membership.' As for elections at the municipal, local and state levels, the provision laid down in Article 58 of the Statutes stipulates: 'As a rule, the lists of candidates shall ensure a minimum 40 per cent representation of one of the sexes, and in any event they shall ensure a minimum one-third representation of one sex. These quotas shall be increased by 5 per cent for each mandate [term of office] until equal representation of both sexes is provided for.' Quotas determined in such a way represent a gradual implementation of equal participation of both sexes in lists of candidates, while at the same time the minimum presence of 'one of the sexes' is set at a relatively high level. The provision regarding quotas as formulated by the United List could be interpreted as a binding provision with regard to which negotiation is impossible and which cannot be arbitrarily altered.

In the 1996 election also, most Slovene political parties resorted to formulating statements of support for the equal representation of women in important political decision-making bodies.[17] Even in 1997, some political parties still failed to include in their policies the fundamental principles regarding support for equal opportunities for men and women; what is more, some parties have publicly voiced their opposition to quotas.[18] These parties perceive quotas first and foremost as a means of oppression and not as a means of temporary compensation for the current state of affairs in the political sphere with women starting from a worse position than their colleagues.

During the discussion on quotas within parties in the run-up to the 1996 election another heated discussion arose regarding legally determined quotas. Even during the discussion of the Law on Political Parties, which was proceeding through parliament in 1994, proposals arose to the effect that parties should in fact ensure equal participation of both sexes in lists of candidates. During the first reading, the conclusion was adopted that the author of the bill 'while preparing the bill for the second reading should examine the possibility of the inclusion of a provision, binding upon political parties, to the effect that they should ensure in their lists of candidates that neither of the sexes shall be represented by less than a 40 per cent share'.[19] In the second and third readings this proposal did not attract the necessary support, and for this reason the Law on Political Parties, adopted in October 1994, contains only the provision that in its statutes a party shall stipulate 'the means of ensuring equal opportunities for both sexes in determining candidates for elections'.[20]

This provision was interpreted in different ways by the parties, and most of them did not implement it. Most frequently, they included a general definition in their statutes: 'In determining candidates for the above-mentioned elections equal opportunities for the participation of both sexes should be ensured.'[21] Of course, these and similar definitions cannot be understood as determining the means of ensuring equal opportunities for candidates in the selection procedure. What is at stake is the fact that the parties circumvented the legal provision by adopting a strategy of verbal support for enhanced encouragement of women in politics which is not legally binding. This is another reason why, just over a year before the third election to the National Assembly, discussions arose in public about how to force parties by means of legal provisions to put into practice in politics the declared commitment to equal participation of men and women. Together with the realization that party policies are particularly inclined to give verbal support to women in politics, this was also prompted by the dissatisfaction with the current proportion of women in important posts in politics, parliament or both, and, last but not least, by the forthcoming elections to the National Assembly.

The most radical demands were voiced by the members of the United List of Social Democrats. In December 1995, the bill to amend the Law on Political Parties was submitted to the National Assembly, authored by a group of MPs (most of them from the ULSD). The proposal for the amendment of Article 1 of the law, signed by the women MPs of the Slovene People's Party and the MP representing the Hungarian ethnic minority, contained concrete demands: 'For the 1996 election to the National Assembly and for the following local elections, a party shall in its lists of candidates ensure a minimum one-third representation of one sex. This share shall be increased each subsequent year by five per cent until equal representation of both sexes is ensured.'[22]

The bill also included a form of sanction, stipulating that a party which increases the share of women in the parliamentary group by ten percentage points shall receive an additional financial reward.[23] In its passage through parliament, the bill was not adopted.

From a theoretical point of view, the proposal for the legal enforcement of quotas is almost 'perfect'. It contains precisely defined quotas, which should be gradually attained; quotas are legally binding upon all the parties, and they also include positive sanctions, thereby indirectly forcing the parties to put women in 'winnable' electoral units. On the other hand, the proposal does suffer some weaknesses at the level of implementation. Above all, in the electoral system in Slovenia, it makes it possible, along with the forced acceptance of quotas, for the lists of candidates to be drawn up in such a way as to prevent women from being elected to the National Assembly despite being included into the lists. The substantial damage that may be caused to the idea of approximately equal representation in parliament should force very careful consideration of whether legally determined quotas, compulsory for all the parties, are completely justifiable: perhaps legally binding incentives for a larger number of female candidates in the lists would be more appropriate.

A second attempt at a transition from verbal formulations of support to the equal participation of women in politics and then to the establishment of a genuine equality of participation by women is furnished by the proposal of woman MP from the LDS for a binding interpretation of the above-mentioned Article 19 of the Law on Political Parties. The proposal for a binding interpretation of Article 5 of that law, submitted in May 1996 in the name of the commission, states:

> The method of ensuring equal opportunities for both sexes in determining candidates for elections under Article 19, Item 4 means that the party statutes shall determine precisely the procedures and measures for the determination of candidates, and for this reason a mere summary or a mere statement or affirming the principle of equal opportunities is not sufficient without a specific and precise definition of procedures and measures.[24]

The purpose of the binding interpretation is to give substance to the expression 'the means of ensuring'. This binding interpretation was not adopted either. The National Assembly thereby clearly took up a position against further specifying the strategies of positive discrimination.

Irrespective of the above, the fact remains that if we truly wish to attain at least approximately equal participation of men and women in lists of candidates, these demands should be clearly stated. For example, in accordance with its policy, a party shall determine:

(1) its understanding of the equal opportunities for both sexes;

(2) how it will ensure a certain proportional presence of women in lists of candidates, which it deems to be optimal;

(3) in what period of time it can implement this.

If the law provided for such definitions in the party statutes, differences between parties over the issue of women's politics (the issue of equal representation of men and women) would become more transparent. The law, on the other hand, would not force parties into complying with a unified system of determination of quotas for the minimum participation of both sexes, and would at the same time offer a challenge to them in the form of competing for the votes of female voters.

By drawing attention to the provision which should commit the parties to make transparent their policy towards the issue of 'equal presence', we wish to underline the fact that the quota provisions can be successful only if certain related conditions are met as well. Quotas by themselves cannot solve the issue of wider participation of women in politics and in parliament. The basic condition necessary for the quotas to be able to play their role is a political atmosphere favourably inclined towards the equality of men and women (both within the parties and in society as a whole).

Above all, it is true that quotas can exert an influence on the increased opportunities for the election of women in the conditions of proportional representation with a party list of candidates – that is, when their participation in the election is collective and not individual. When women stand in electoral units individually, they have smaller chances of being elected – even if the quota provisions are enforced – than if they stand in electoral units in party lists of candidates.

NOTES

1. See Carole Pateman, *The Disorder of Women* (Cambridge: Polity, 1989), p.214.
2. The concept of 'unfinished democracy' may be found in the works of Scandinavian feminist authors: Elina Haavio-Mannila *et al.*, *Unfinished Democracy: Women in Nordic Politics* (Oxford: Pergamon Press, 1985). The term 'male democracy' is also quite widespread and debated by many women authors: see Mita Castle-Kanerova, 'Czech and Slovak Federative Republic', in Chris Corrin (ed.), *Superwomen and the Double Burden* (London: Scarlet Press, 1992); and N. Funk and M. Mueller (eds.), *Gender Politics and Postcommunism* (New York: Routledge, 1993).
3. Data on the percentage of women in important party bodies for 1993 are based on the publication *Women in Political Parties*, published by the Government Office for Women's Politics (Ljubljana, 1994), Nos.11 and 12); those for 1997 form part of the material for the analysis of the 1997 election, undertaken by the Office for Women's Politics and submitted to the Office by the parties themselves. It is interesting to note that data on the percentage of women members of political parties by D. Zajc in his contribution, 'Some Problems of Representation in the Process of Slovene Political Transition' (unpublished, 1997), differ from ours, even though, as in the present author's case, they were furnished by the parties themselves: see D. Zajc, 'Some Problems of Representation in the Process of Slovene Political Transition', p.8.
4. At the party's second Congress in 1992, the provision was adopted to the effect that in both elected and appointed party bodies at the national level 'no sex may be represented by less than one-third of candidates', *LDS Statutes* (Ljubljana, 1992), p.2.
5. Their statutes also include a provision to the effect that lists of candidates for parliamentary elections shall ensure a minimum of 40 per cent representation of one sex, and in any event a minimum one-third representation. These quotas are supposed to increase by five per cent for each term of office: see *The ULSD Congress Documents* (Slovenj Gradec, 1996), p.90. The formulation in the ULSD statutes is somewhat awkward: taken literally, it would mean that one of the sexes is always represented by at least a 40 per cent share. It would be much more straightforward if the wording were that both sexes shall be represented by at least a 40 per cent share of candidates included on the lists of candidates.
6. Article 19 of the *Law on Political Parties* stipulates that a party shall lay down in its statutes 'a procedure and a body determining candidates for elections to Parliament and for the President of the Republic, together with candidates for elections to local community bodies' (see the *Official Gazette of the Republic of Slovenia*, 7 Oct. 1994). Article 43 of the *Law on Elections* stipulates that 'A political party shall determine the candidates in accordance with a procedure laid down by internal rules. A list of candidates shall be determined in a secret ballot': 'Election Regulations', *The Official Gazette of the Republic of Slovenia* (Ljubljana, 1992), p.17.
7. In the 1992 election, a total of 1,488,966 voters had the right to vote; 782,4333 or 52.54 per cent were women: *The 1993 Statistical Yearbook*, pp.50–51.)
8. In the 1996 election, a total of 1,539,987 voters had the right to vote; 806,742 or 52.38 per cent were women: *Statistical Data 93/1997* (Ljubljana: Statistical Office), pp.28–9.
9. Data based on the publication of the Office for Women's Politics, *Women in Political Parties* (Ljubljana, 1994).

10. Data on the percentage of women party members are based on parties' own assessments, while data on the percentage of women in lists of candidates and in party parliamentary groups are official figures.

11. This may be observed in the programme of the Slovene People's Party – the second largest party – which stipulates that within the framework of family policy it shall uphold, *inter alia*, 'a tax policy which will undoubtedly favour families with several children; a solution to pension legislation which will take motherhood into account; a gradual extension of maternity leave, the activities of the mass media encouraging the values of parenthood, marriage and family' (*Slovene People's Party Programme*, p.16).

12. For an additional explanation, one may take account of some additional facts, which were particularly evident in the Liberal Democracy of Slovenia, the winner of the last election (from 23.46 per cent, its share increased to 27.01 per cent). In lists of candidates there were 13.6 per cent women (compared with 9.3 per cent in the 1992 election), while the proortion in its parliamentary group was cut by half. This was to a large extent the result of strong competition on the part of their male party colleagues within individual electoral districts. This is the party in which the largest number of former ministers and MPs stood as candidates.

13. See Robert Darcy and Susan Welch, writing in Janet Clark, *Women, Elections and Representation* (Lincoln, NE and London: University of Nebraska Press, 1994), p.173. In the USA, a discussion about democracy being under threat is under way, because the share of those re-elected has again exceeded 90 per cent.

14. An analysis of individual parties shows that 15 out of 22 former MPs (68.2 per cent) stood as LDS candidates, eight out of ten (80 per cent) as SPP candidates, three out of four (75 per cent) as Social Democratic Party candidates, 12 out of 15 (80 per cent) as Slovene Christian Democrats candidates and ten out of 14 (71 per cent as the United List of Social Democrats candidates. Of 15 former Liberal Democracy of Slovenia MPs who stood again, ten (66.67 per cent) were re-elected; of three Social Democratic Party MPs who stood again, two (66.67 per cent) were re-elected; of eight former People's Party MPs who stood again, half of them were re-elected; out of 12 former Christian Democrat MPs who stood again, a third were re-elected. The probability of re-election was therefore the highest in the case of Liberal Democracy of Slovenia and Social Democratic Party of Slovenia candidates.

15. Bearing in mind the fact that the male and female representatives of minorities were re-elected in the previous term also, it becomes clear that new male and female MPs were left with a very narrow manoeuvring space indeed.

16. J. Siklova substantiates the rejection of quotas in the Czech Republic as follows: 'Through personal experience we know that the establishment of quotas for various social groups or other forms of so-called "positive discrimination", which have been so politically important in the West, often become a tool of oppression of the very groups they were designed to support': see J. Šiklová, 'Are Women in Eastern and Central Europe Conservative?', in Funk and Mueller, *Gender Politics and Postcommunism* (New York: Routledge, 1993), p.79. According to Larisa Lissyutkina, 'Soviet women also do not support the concept of quotas in the democratic elections. Many see quotas as the continuation of the communist regime's practices and privileges': see her 'Soviet Women at the Crossroads of Perestroika', in ibid., p.279.

17. Verbal formulations also include provisions adopted by the SCD at its sixth annual conference on 23 March 1996, when 'a resolution, that is a recommendation of the SCD Council' was adopted, 'in which it is proposed that the SCD Council shall include as many women as possible in lists of candidates for the elections to the National Assembly, while in the national lists at least three women shall be included among the first ten names' (*Republika*, 24 March 1996).

18. The position of the SDP may serve as an example. Its programme, adopted in May 1995, contains the following provision: 'Women should secure by themselves equal access to all functions of decision-making in the country, including the most important ones' (p.21). At its session of 8 February 1996, the Executive Committee of Women Social Democrats within the SDP adopted the position that 'the representation of women in lists of candidates is a party's decision, and that consequently, they were opposed to the enforcement of binding quotas' (*Slovenec*, 9 Feb. 1996).

19. See the record of the 23rd session of the National Assembly of 13 September 1994, *Session Records*, p.495.
20. See Article 19 of the 'Law on Political Parties', *Official Gazette of the RS*, 7 Oct. 1997.
21. See Article 68 of the *SCD Statutes*, adopted at the October 1994 congress, with modifications adopted in April 1995. The provision in the Democratic Party Statutes is similarly formulated, 'By means of regulations and/or the Rules of Procedure from the preceding paragraph of this Article equal opportunities shall be ensured for both sexes in determining candidates for national and local elections' (Article 65 of the *DP Statutes*, adopted in November 1994 and amended in March 1995). A similar provision is contained in the *SPP Statutes*: see Article 52, 'In determining candidates equal opportunities shall be ensured for both sexes'.
22. See *Parliamentary Reports*, 1995, No.55, p.22.
23. Article 2 of the bill stipulates that 'A party which will improve the percentage of women in its parliamentary group by 10 percentage points in comparison with the previous election result is entitled to additional budgetary resources. A party entering Parliament for the first time is entitled to this bonus if it has at least one elected woman MP. Additional financial means shall amount to 5 Tolars per each vote in the women's share of votes cast by the electorate, which shall correspond to the share of women in the parliamentary group. A party which achieves total balance of both sexes of the elected MPs and/or where the difference between the number of female and male MPs does not exceed one acquires the right to 5 additional Tolars per all the votes of the electorate cast for it': *Parliamentary Reports*, 1995, No.55. p.22.
24. *Parliamentary Reports*, 1996, No.22, p.55, and the report on the activities of the Commission for Women's Politics for the period 1992–96 (Ljubljana, Sept. 1996), p.13.

Women's Groups: The Albanian Case

DELINA FICO

The collapse in 1990 of the totalitarian regime, which kept Albanian society under tight control for 45 years, has been followed by deep political and social changes, including the formation and strengthening of women's organizations and movements. Responding to the particular needs of women, which are largely overlooked by policy-makers and absent from public debate, Albanian women's non-governmental organizations (NGOs) have expanded their activities to address women's social, legal and health issues in both urban and rural areas. There are complex processes involved in building a women's movement from scratch, developing alliances among women's groups and with other sectors of society, while grappling with a series of obstacles that range from low awareness of women's rights to the lack of recognition by government authorities of the efforts and the range of roles played by women's groups.

The first voluntary organizations in Albania date from immediately after the country proclaimed its independence from the Ottoman Empire in 1912. Between 1918 and 1925 a number of patriotic cultural, literary and sports associations, societies and federations were formed in the main centres of the newly-born state. Their aim was to promote a strong political and cultural national identity. Part of this picture was formed by associations, clubs and federations of Albanians living abroad, particularly in the United States of America, Romania, Bulgaria and Turkey. One of the most active organizations was 'Sisters Qiriazi', which opened the first school for girls in Albanian in the southern part of the country.

The end of the Second World War left Albania within the area of communist influence. Between 1945 and 1990 Albania was ruled by an increasingly totalitarian self-declared socialist (communist) party-state. Among other things, this meant total repression of most individual freedoms and rights, although they were formally recognized in the Constitution of the People's Socialist Republic of Albania. The Law on Association, number 2362, passed in 1956, imposed total state control on the activities of voluntary organizations. These organizations were considered tools in the hands of Albanian Party of Labour (that is, communist party) propaganda. Between 1960 and 1990 the right to association was expressed through the so-called 'organizations of the masses' which were considered 'transmission wheels between the party and the masses'. The Union of Albanian Women (UAW) was one of these. UAW is an explicit example of the governmentally organized non-governmental organizations (GONGOs), and also of the forced 'voluntary' contribution to the community. Each housing block (the smallest unit in urban areas) and each village had a branch of UAW. A woman could be elected to head the organization, but she had to be either a member of the communist party or a person with very good political biography, which meant no trace of dissent regarding the policies of the party. These small branches concerned themselves with a range of issues regarding the neighbourhood: regulations on when children could play outside, negotiations between spouses in cases of marital problems, keeping the areas around the buildings clean and tidy, and organizing meetings to condemn individuals who manifested pro-Western behaviour. Such behaviour was considered not to match the norms defined by the party about what to say, what music to listen to, how to dress, how many rings to wear. This so-called 'mass organization' was far from a non-profit organization in its goals, structure and activities. UAW was not fuelled by the voluntary actions of individuals or communities: it collected a symbolic membership fee, but was funded mainly by the state budget. The positions held at the higher levels of UAW were a step towards a leadership position in the communist party.

The Rebirth of Women's Groups

In December 1990, following the students' protests, the first opposition party was formed and in April 1991 the first semi-free elections were held. In March 1992 the opposition, represented by the Democratic Party, won. The new parliament approved a set of Fundamental Laws in April 1991, to replace the Constitution, which was not valid in the entirely different political, economic and social context. The articles of these laws enshrined freedom of speech and of association.

The first years following the political changes in Albania were extremely difficult. The country faced a harsh economy and social crises due to the poverty inherited from the communist past and to the inability of the Democratic Party government to revitalize production. The political milieu focused only on blaming the communist past for the current situation, failing to discuss ideas and take effective measures to improve conditions. The introduction of the multiparty system and principles of a market economy, and the recognition of the individual rights to freedom of movement, religion, speech and property created for the first time in 45 years a space for the individual and group interests to be considered, identified and defended. In this context, the first women's groups in Albania started as a group of people around a common interest, as a need for group identity and solidarity. They acknowledged the lack of recognition of women as a social group and of their particular needs. It should be noted here that a gender perspective was totally absent from the public discussion about wrongdoings of the past or projections for the future. It was very rare to hear about the abuse and hardships that women had gone through during the totalitarian regime – not only women who served time in prison and internment camps, but also women in the workplace and within their own homes. The League of Former Politically Persecuted Women (now the 'Revival' Association) was established to represent this group of women and to assist them in the process of reintegration into society.

As early as 1991 the Union of Albanian Women was dissolved. The Independent Forum of Albanian Women (IFAW) was founded from some of the most progressive women that had joined UAW in the last years of its existence. IFAW is today one of the most successful women's NGOs in Albania. The Democratic Forum of Albanian Women was established right after the creation of the Democratic Party (DP). This organization considered itself a part of the DP, a situation that has not changed a great deal to date. In the same spirit, the Forum of Republican Women and some other party-affiliated women's groups were created. These groups remained deeply linked with their parties and were active especially during election time to mobilize women to vote for the party. These party-affiliated women's organizations collect membership fees, but are mainly financed by their respective parties. Recently, some of them have been incorporated separately as NGOs, a step that is aimed particularly at securing funding from outside donors and greater independence for their leaders.Two of the first women's NGOs, the 'Refleksione' Women's Association and the 'Useful to Albanian Women' Association (UAW) started in 1991–92 with the initiative of small groups of professional women in the capital, Tirana. Initially they looked more like consciousness-raising groups, but rapidly developed into advocacy organizations, educating women about their rights and trying to make their cause visible in the media and to the government.

From the outset, women's NGOs in Albania were born to respond to the needs of women in the country. During early 1990, UAW and IFAW served as channels to distribute humanitarian aid to Albanian families. 'Refleksione' was involved in activities related to family planning and awareness of women and children's rights. Meanwhile, the technical and financial support of foreign and international governmental and non-profit organizations for the first women's NGOs in Albania was significant from the early days. Church-based Swiss organizations provided funding for UAW, while Italian NGOs and the United Nations Development Programme (UNDP) supported IFAW. This support has been crucial in enhancing the ability of these organizations to reach a greater number of women and diversify their activities. The interaction of women's NGOs in

Albania with foreign organizations has not suffered from fears of intervention or imposing agendas from the outside, an issue often raised by some women's groups in Eastern and Central Europe.

However, during 1991–94 the number and the visibility of the women's NGOs remained very low. This was common for the entire third sector in Albania. Albanians suffered from what some researchers call 'fear of association'.[1] Having for a long time been forced to live in a collective manner, they were eager to enjoy individual freedom, which they wrongly perceived as threatened by any kind of associative effort. Ideas of collective action and voluntarism were severely damaged because of their misuse by totalitarian propaganda. The struggle for the economic survival of their families was an important factor underlying the lack of interest and willingness among Albanians to contribute time and resources to NGOs.

Working Together

In 1994–95 the number of women's NGOs in Albania started to increase, a process that continues. Today there are about 55 women's NGOs incorporated in the country, according to the Women's Centre, Tirana. While the earlier established NGOs developed into larger multi-purpose organizations, smaller organizations focused on more specific group interests, such as business and professional women, disabled women, artists, and rural women. Some of the NGOs expanded their activities outside Tirana and a few locally based groups were founded in other regions: the Businesswomen's Association in Vlorë is one example.

In 1994 the 'Gender in Development' (GID) project of the UNDP started in Albania. This project played a pioneering role in bringing Albanian women's NGOs together to work, in introducing an international perspective to their work, and in establishing links with other women's NGOs outside the country. In August 1994 the Women's Centre (WCT) was established, initially as a project of the 'Refleksione' Women's Association funded by the Open Society Foundation for Albania. The mission of the WCT was to provide a space where women's groups could meet and share their ideas and initiate common activities. It was also intended to collect and share information on gender issues in Albania and abroad. WCT worked closely with the GID programme during 1994–95 in fulfilling its mission. As a first step, twice-weekly meetings of the women's NGOs were held at the WCT. Politically independent women's organizations and the party-affiliated women's groups took part in these meetings.

This was the very first time groups from opposing political sectors of the society were coming together around the same table and discussing issues of common concern. From the beginning there was a willingness on the part of all the women's groups to focus on women's concerns and not to let political differences interfere with the group dynamics. Various important initiatives grew from these meetings. On 8 March 1995, 14 women's NGOs held the first press conference on women. The event was an attempt to make women's issues and women's groups visible in the media. The twice-weekly meetings at the WCT gradually designed an informal coalition of women's groups in Albania. Two important common projects of this coalition were the Women's Legal Group (WLG) and the Women's Health Group (WHG). These were groups of professionals, respectively lawyers and doctors, representing different women's NGOs, but working together on women's issues. In a way they were task forces of the Women's NGOs focused on specific projects. The Women's Legal Group and the Women's Health Group had the support of nearly all the women's NGOs existing at that time in Albania and were coordinated by the Women's Centre.

The first successful effort of the WLG was to lobby for changes in the new Labour Code. It was the very first time that women's NGOs in Albania went through a lobbying process. This effort was an exercise in democracy for members of women's NGOs. The WLG reviewed the draft of the Labour Code, discussed the provisions regarding women, consulted foreign lawyers on these topics, and designed a set of recommendations aiming to address specifically women's rights in the workplace. The WLG met the Legal Commission of parliament, participated in its meetings and presented its own suggestions. Representatives of the women's NGOs met the women Members of Parliament, numbering seven at that time, informed them about their efforts to influence the new Labour Code and gained their support. Consequently, the parliamentary Legal Commission endorsed most of the suggestions and they were passed by parliament.

Articles on sexual harassment were added to the new Labour Code, following the proposal of the women's groups, and it was the very first time that the concept of sexual harassment was introduced into Albanian legislation.

The WLG proceeded to work on a series of other ideas. In late 1995 this group was incorporated in Tirana district as an NGO. It aimed to increase the independence of the group in terms of management and to develop a more rigorous profile as a professional entity. The consequences of this step are considerable for, as the link of the WLG to women's NGOs weakened, their members were no longer obliged to report to the NGO which they represented. This meant that they were not now speaking on behalf of 12 women's organizations, and this diminished the WLG's influence in the lobbying efforts. In 1996 the Women's Bar Association was established on the initiative of the most active members of the WLG.

In late 1995 the other task force of the women's NGOs, the Women's Health Group, developed a programme of projects to be accomplished. The group developed a series of TV programmes on women's health issues, which were shown on the single state television channel. The important point was that these programmes were produced by Albanian women, using their own experience, and were not the usual foreign programme translated from other languages, with no perspectives on the specific issues and circumstances relevant to women in Albania. Video tapes of these programmes were used as training materials in health education for women in both urban and rural areas. The WCT and the Albanian Research Centre for Health, today the 'Health for All' Foundation, coordinated the activities of the group.

During 1995–97 co-operation among women's NGOs in Albania grew stronger. As mentioned above, this was an informal coalition that worked on the basis of projects. All women's groups insisted that their co-operation should not develop into a formal structure, but remain informal. The legacy of the UAW, a large, extremely hierarchical structure controlled and directed from the top, was a burden that scared women away from federated or umbrella organizations. The women's NGOs were eager to preserve their independence and their own voice. The coalition was a flexible structure. Some organizations were more active, some new groups came and some older groups were not present all the time. In 1996 this process was partly related to political developments in the country and the positioning of the WCT and some of the women's NGOs against the increasing authoritarian power of the president, Sali Berisha. Thus, the League of Democratic Women (the group affiliated with the Democratic Party), was no longer in practical terms part of the coalition, although it never presented this position officially to the rest of the women's groups.

The major international event pertaining to women's issues – and mostly those in preparation to the Beijing Conference – created a momentum for better co-operation among women's groups. Before the Conference, the GID programme and the WCT organized a round table with the potential sponsors, where women's NGOs presented their activities and their plans for the future. Eventually, 12 Albanian women representing a dozen women's groups were able to take part at the NGO Forum of the Fourth World Conference on Women, Huairou, China, in August–September 1995. This was a first time ever that a large number of Albanian NGOs had taken part in an international conference, and for the Albanian women's groups this event marked a turning-point. They enjoyed the solidarity of women's groups from all over the world, felt empowered from the awareness that so many women share their struggle for the advancement of women, and established contacts with organizations and experts on various issues of concern to women. Albanian women's NGOs coordinated by the WCT produced a report on women's NGOs in Albania and contributed to the Report on the Status of Women prepared by the Albanian government for the Beijing Conference. This effort marked the beginning of a dialogue with the Department on Women's Issues in the Ministry of Social Protection, Emigration and Employment – a dialogue that was not an easy one, however.

Having lived through 45 years of total government control, individuals involved in the NGOs distrusted the governmental structures. On the other hand, the first democratically-elected government did not do a great deal to dissolve the hostility. The heavily corrupt government of the Democratic Party (1992–97) showed signs of increasing political intolerance and violation of human rights, failing to take into consideration the well-established organizations when issues of public concern were discussed. At the same time, the government promoted the creation of NGOs which would opportunistically support and rubber-stamp government decisions. When it by chance happened, the government's recognition of the existence and work of NGOs was more a reflection of the pressure from abroad on the government to act according to the model of the democratic countries in their relations with the voluntary sector. The co-operation of the women's NGOs' coalition with the government structures came to a halt during 1996 when the WCT and some of the women's groups publicly opposed the political violence before, during and after the parliamentary elections of May 1996.

In an attempt to join forces with other groups interested in the empowerment of women in Albania, women's NGOs worked on a project basis with other organizations. It is interesting to note here that the Family Planning Association, one of the best-established and most efficient NGOs in Albania, has not played an active part in the women's NGOs' coalition. Yet the coalition worked closely with the Family Planning Association in lobbying to keep abortion free in Albania. Abortion was banned during the totalitarian regime; in 1991, a governmental decree legalized abortion; in 1996, the Ministry of Health drafted a law on abortion and sent it to parliament for approval. The parliament rejected the draft, saying that it was too liberal. Women Members of Parliament voted for this option also – out of ignorance, so they said. The WLG worked on amendments to the draft law, women's NGOs met the expert group of the Ministry of Health, and all of them – except for the Baha'i women's group – expressed their support for keeping abortion legal in Albania. The Family Planning Association prepared a file with materials on the abortion law in other countries and distributed it among Members of Parliament. Women's organizations also lobbied the women MPs to earn their support for the second draft of the law.

Parliament approved the new abortion law, although it did not embody all the proposals of the women's groups, so that, according to the existing law, abortion in Albania is legal with some minor restrictions.

In an attempt to increase the presence of women in the public life, in 1996 women's NGOs in partnership with the Society for Democratic Culture developed a campaign to promote women's participation in elections, both as voters and as candidates. The campaign started with women meeting in a number of regions to discuss issues that they wanted to see on the political agenda, including education on how to use the electoral process to further their programme, and aimed at lobbying political parties to include more women in their lists of candidates for parliament. The interaction with the political parties was almost impossible, since most of them could not see the need to discuss issues concerning women during the election campaign.

A poster was prepared with the names and data on all the women candidates, urging women to vote for women. The campaign raised women's awareness of the need and the opportunities to play a more active part in political decision-making. Women's groups wanted to continue to work on this issue, but the political development during and after the general election of 26 May 1996 changed the focus of their activity. Fraud and irregularities largely marred these elections, and escalating political violence followed. On 28 May the opposition organized a rally to protest against the manipulations and the government forces tried forcibly to stop the demonstration. Women, old and young, were beaten and detained by the police. Meanwhile, women candidates from the opposition were assaulted during the electoral campaign. Immediately after these events, 12 women's NGOs published a press release to protest against the violence during and after the elections, particularly against women candidates and against women in general.

In September 1996, 14 women's groups protested in the media against the harassment of women journalists and women activists of NGOs, by the state-run media, some of which had launched vicious attacks against leaders of women's NGOs. Some other members of the women's NGOs' coalition were pressured by their employers in government institutions not to become involved with the coalition. In a situation of increasingly authoritarian government, women's groups were among the very few NGOs to stand publicly, not from a partisan perspective, against the political pressure and the violations of human rights. During 1997, when Albania went through a deep political, economic and moral crisis linked to the collapse of pyramid selling and investment schemes, women's NGOs joined forces with other civic organizations to call for the restoration of public order and against political violence.

Challenges and Opportunities

Surely Albania is taking part in what is called a global 'association revolution'.[2] The women's NGOs, as well as part of the third sector, are increasing and becoming players in issues related to women in Albania. Since 1996 some of them are providing services to women through projects such as the Counselling Centre for Women and Girls, which assists victims of domestic violence, Family Planning Clinics and the Information Centre for Drug and Alcohol Addicts. Still their initiatives do not even come close to fulfilling the needs of women and children in Albania for social and health services. It is not expected that they should carry the task of entirely providing these services, but in conditions where the state fails to offer such services, the need is huge and the resources that NGOs have are extremely limited.

This leads to one of the major concerns regarding the NGOs in Albania, including women's NGOs: the sustainability of their programmes. This is a concern shared by most of the NGOs in Eastern and Central Europe. So far, foreign donors, private foundations, foreign non-profit organizations and UN programmes have largely funded the Albanian women's NGOs. After 1997 the share of foreign aid going to NGOs in Albania is increasing. The reasons for such a process are the same as those analysed by Estell[3] for other developing countries: NGOs provide trustworthy information, they have low administration costs (the higher wages are still less costly than the losses due to state corruption and ineffective structures) and they can operate in politically sensitive areas where government authorities would be suspect.

In Albania we can add that the political instability makes difficult the continuation of foreign aid programmes at the governmental level. Moreover, assisting NGOs is perceived by foreign donors as a way to promote the democratization of the country by increasing the participation of citizens in dealing with issues of public concern. But, depending entirely – or even largely – on foreign donors' money raises concerns that are vital for the identity and the sustainability of the women's NGOs. First, it questions the authenticity of these groups as structures supported by the willingness of women to dedicate resources to their own organizations. In a poor country like Albania, where the majority of women struggle for economic survival, the membership fees are insignificant and individual women are very rarely in the position to donate money or services in kind to NGOs. On the other hand, the women's NGOs have not worked enough with the new entrepreneurs to educate them about giving financial support to NGOs.

The situation becomes more complex when we consider the fact that the tax-exempt status of private donations is not yet clearly regulated in Albania. Furthermore, in a situation where the collection of taxes is at a rudimentary stage, it is hard to predict what the outcome might have been had such regulations been in place. Aware of the gap in terms of funding for NGOs within the country, some women's groups have developed income-earning activities, such as publishing houses, printing houses, greenhouses and so on, to fund their programmes.

Secondly, the fact that foreign donors are the main source of funding might promote divisiveness among women's groups, as researchers have noted for other countries of Eastern and Central Europe. In Albania this trend has been entwined with political ramifications. Attacks in some Albanian newspapers against some of the most successful women's NGOs, accusing them of links with the communist past and of mismanagement of funds, are fuelled by an organization close to the Democratic Party. Once the DP lost power, this organization lost its privileged access to funding sources channelled through government. Competing for funds from foreign donors present in Albania, the organization chose to throw mud at other women's groups, a situation which was very sad to witness. The risk of promoting divisiveness has been noted even by donor organizations. Some of them have recently changed their strategies to give priority to projects that are developed and implemented by groups of organizations. Two new coalitions of Albanian women's NGOs, *Millennium* and the *Federation of Albanian Women*, are attempting to take advantage of this strategy.

The new government that came to power after the elections of 19 June 1997 seems to be more open to broader participation by different actors in governing the country; it also recognizes the role of NGOs in this process. In this context women's groups have widened the areas of co-operation with the governmental structures that deal with women's issues. This includes delivering a larger share of the foreign aid channelled through the government as grants to the women's NGOs. In a way, the government is recognizing the fact that women's groups have acquired expertise in the area of women's legal, social and health issues. And if one looks at the general picture, it seems as though the women's NGOs are doing well: they are active, their number is increasing, and their activities are diversifying. But when one looks at the difficult problems that Albanian women are facing today, ranging from prostitution and trafficking in women, poverty, unemployment, lack of adequate health and social services, domestic violence and lack of participation in decision-making, one wonders what that says for the role and the impact that women's groups have in the everyday life of Albanian women.

In the first place, this reflects the fact that women's NGOs, in common with the entire emerging NGO sector in Albania, have not yet developed into a large and powerful movement capable of imposing changes on the society. Secondly, this also raises questions about the ideology and strategy of the women's movement in Albania. The immediate picture is more that of a number of women's groups trying to respond to the current needs of women in segments of the society. For all the networking efforts so far, there is no clarity and cohesiveness in terms of common long-term strategies for the political, economic and social advancement of women in the country. The women's movement has a long way to go to become an inclusive movement of women from all over the country and from all social strata, aware of their rights and mobilized to fight for them at the community, local and national level.

Concluding Note

I have attempted to present here a sketch of the rebirth and the growth of the women's organizations in Albania. As a founding member of the 'Refleksione' Women's Association and the first coordinator of the Women's Centre, I was part of this process as it moved ahead rapidly. For all of us who were there from the beginning, in starting women's groups, developing the first projects and establishing the first service Centres, these were our contribution to the overwhelming changes that our country was going through. It was also our way of transforming ourselves, learning democracy, building democracy in our own territory, and building the movement and the experience of working within it. We learned to listen to one another, to respect the differences and not to let them destroy our coalition, to plan a campaign and implement it, to lobby parliament and work with the government while maintaining our own independent view. And this all came from within ourselves. Most of us had not read feminist books, we did not know about sisterhood, non-hierarchical structures, collegial meetings and decisions by consensus. But that is how we made decisions in our organizations and in our coalition. We valued friendship and solidarity above all. We were never angry with one another, even when we disagreed. We tried to help the new organizations, share information and assist each other with everything. There were misunderstandings and there were free-riders. But we survived and build our culture of support and respect for one another. As a first step we are building a better place for ourselves.The huge challenge ahead of us remains to make Albania a better place for everyone.

NOTES

1. P.D. Hall, 'Historical Perspective on Nonprofit Organiszations', in *The Jossey-Bass Handbook of Nonprofit Leadership and Management* (San Francisco, CA: Jossey-Bass, 1994).
2. Lester M. Salamon, 'The Rise of the Nonprofit Sector', *Foreign Affairs*, July–Aug. 1994, p.109.
3. James Estell (ed.), *The Nonprofit Sector in International Perspective: Studies in Comparative Culture and Policy* (Oxford: Oxford University Press, 1989), p.22.

Violence Against Women:
International Standards, Polish Reality

URSZULA NOWAKOWSKA

In considering the work of the Women's Rights Centre on violence against women, within an international framework of women's human rights work, the particular legal and social barriers to the recognition and eradication of this social problem in Poland become apparent. The changing political climate in Poland has adversely affected some of the progressive measures which had been struggled for by women's activities in this field. In measuring Polish reality against international standards, despite other major social changes in Poland, violence against women is still not recognized as the problem that it is. Changes in jurdisprudence, law-making and sentencing could all be made to improve the negative situations in which women who suffer violence generally find themselves. The limitation of official data acts as another barrier in estimating statistics on crimes of violence in the home. The 'letter of the law' and the 'law in practice' remain two different things when issues of violence against women are considered. It is apparent that attitudes are as important as legislation, and indeed if violence against women is considered insignificant they are treated differently from other crimes. Comparisons of progressive language in international human rights documents with the improvement at the national level in Poland show the gap between verbal commitments and reality. As violence against women still constitutes a challenge to the national and international communities, political will and concrete remedies are required.

Violence Against Women as a Human Rights Issue

The long struggle for women's rights as human rights gained momentum in the early part of the 1990s along with the ending of the cold war. The Global Campaign for Women's Human Rights, launched by the Centre for Women's Global Leadership Institute in New Jersey, was certainly an important vehicle in putting forward the issue of women's human rights and violence against women. The petition, calling upon the 1995 World Conference to comprehensively address women's human rights at every level of its proceedings, and to recognize gender-based violence as 'a violation of human rights requiring immediate action' was translated into 23 languages and gathered half a million signatures from 124 countries.

The critical momentum for women's human rights work was the UN Conference on Human Rights held in Vienna in 1993. The language embraced in the Vienna Declaration and Programme of Action has been a great step forward in integrating women's rights into the human rights agenda. It states: 'The human rights of women and the girl-child are an inalienable, integral and indivisible part of human rights.'

In December 1993 the United Nation General Assembly adopted the Declaration on the Elimination of Violence Against Women. It is the first international human rights instrument exclusively and implicitly to address the issue of violence against women. It affirms that violence against women constitutes a violation of the rights and fundamental freedoms of women and impairs or nullifies their enjoyment of these rights and freedoms. The Declaration defines violence against women as 'any act of gender-based violence that results in, or is likely to result in, physical, sexual or psychological harm or suffering to women, including threats of such acts, coercion or arbitrary deprivation of liberty, whether occurring in public or in private life'. Recognition that violence against women constitutes a violation of basic human rights of women regardless of who the perpetrator is (the state or a private actor) opens a new dimension in the human rights discourse. It is also worth noting that the Vienna Declaration, the Programme of Action and the UN Declaration Against Violence Against Women affirmed that, in cases of conflict between women's human rights and cultural or religious practices, the human rights of women must prevail.

Acknowledgment, by most of the governments and the UN system, that violence against women is not a private matter, but a pervasive human rights problem requiring state intervention, resulted in further actions. On 4 March 1994 the Human Rights Commission adopted the resolution (1994/45) in which the Special Rapporteur on Violence Against Women, its Causes and Consequences was appointed. The work of the special rapporteur has increased the visibility of the issue of violence against women in the international arena, but we should be aware that not all governments take her work and recommendations seriously. For instance, the report and recommendations prepared by the Special Rapporteur, after her visit to Poland and some other countries in the region, were ignored by the Polish government, and only through the work of NGOs was the report translated into Polish and popularized.

The achievements of the Vienna Conference were confirmed and further developed in the Beijing Platform of Action adopted at the IV UN Conference on Women held in Beijing, in September 1995. Violence against women and women's human rights were identified as the two of 12 critical areas of concern which constitute the main obstacles to the advancement of women. Governments agreed, among other things, to adopt and implement national legislation aimed at providing women with adequate legal and institutional measures to protect them from all forms of gender-based violence. They agreed to set up and support the establishment of shelters for battered women and children, of legal aid and other services for women and girls affected by violence, and of counselling and rehabilitation centres for violent men. Governments also pledged to adopt all appropriate measures to challenge gender-stereotyped images of women and men, often degrading women and presenting them as subordinate to men, and also to encourage non-stereotyped, balanced and diverse images of women in the media and in the field of education.

International Standards and Polish Reality

There is no doubt that over the past five years there has been considerable progress in addressing the issue of violence against women, particularly at the international level. Violence against women is no longer regarded as a private matter: it has been internationally recognized as a pervasive human rights problem. So the time has come to ask ourselves whether this international recognition has improved the lives of Polish women who have fallen victims to violence, and whether these internationally recognized standards and related government commitments have been realized in practice at the national level. Have they made difference in everyday reality?

Despite other major social changes, violence against women are still not adequately recognized as a serious social problem in Poland. It still remains hidden, surrounded by taboos, and marked by a strong tradition of shame and guilt in the case of disclosure, especially in small villages and towns. Polish society continues to accept powerful stereotypes about women's and men's 'traditional' roles in family life, and expectations about the appropriate or acceptable response to 'inappropriate' behaviour by women. Polish folklore still contains such sayings as 'A husband who does not beat his wife does not love her' and 'If a husband does not beat his wife her liver rots'.

Women who are victims of domestic violence or rape have very limited access to psychological counselling and legal assistance. The provision of shelters for abused women is severely inadequate. At the present time, a system of specialized assistance and therapy for women victims of violence has not yet been developed. There are several shelters for homeless women and mothers with small children run by the Church where women can escape violent relationships, but these shelters do not deal specifically with violence. Staff members who run them are often themselves abusive, accusing women of being provocative and teaching them be more docile, the better to satisfy men's needs. Women in these shelters usually do not get the support and assistance they need, and often have to obey abusive rules depriving them of their fundamental human rights.

There have been, however, some significant and positive changes in recent years. The issue of violence against women is now more present in the media. For over four years the government anti-alcoholism agency has designed a programme to combat domestic violence through the administration of a free hotline for victims of domestic violence, and domestic violence programmes are also run by local anti-alcoholism agencies all over Poland. In addition, there exist an increasing number of women's NGOs working on issues of violence against women. The government's anti-alcoholism agency launched a big media campaign on domestic violence in November 1997 and declared November a month against domestic violence. There were many TV and radio programmes as well as articles in local and national newspapers on the issue. Several newspapers published the telephone numbers of non-profit organizations providing services for victims of violence. Posters and billboards were visible in many public spaces and in the streets of big cities. The Department for Family and Women's Affairs of the previous government prepared a programme to deal with violence against women which was incorporated in the Programme of Action to promote women up to the year 2000. Another government programme, 'Against Violence: Equal Chances', was developed by the Bureau for Family and Women's Affairs and co-financed by the UNDP. Under the programme, ten regional centres providing comprehensive assistance to victims of violence were to be established and the staff for these facilities were to be trained.

Meanwhile, there occurred a change of government and the small progress that could be observed was halted. The new minister for family affairs refused to recognize even the very existence of the problem of violence against women. He criticized the campaign against domestic violence as aimed against the family and as irrelevant, since, according to the minister, 'Polish husbands are kind and they treat their wives gently'. One should not consider this statement as a slip of the ministerial tongue, since the government also decided not to enforce the national Plan of Action for the Advancement of Women adopted by the previous government as a follow-up to the Beijing conference, and to abandon the implementation of another programme, 'Against Violence Against Women: Equal Chances'. The minister criticized the programme as aimed at distorting families and presenting bad images of Polish men. He also questioned the prevalence of violence against women, arguing that men are victims as well and added that by portraying men as perpetrators women might be discouraged from getting married.

In his report on the situation of Polish families there was simply no mention of violence against women. In the chapter on violence – the shortest in the report – the only kind of violence mentioned is violence against children. The 'new–old' approach of Minister Kazimierz Kapera towards violence against women, and domestic violence in particular, has been also reflected in the way some sections of the media have presented this issue. According to Polish law, radio and television must respect so-called 'Christian values', and the minister is the former head of the Movement of Catholic Families. There have been several articles and TV programmes in which women were presented as the perpetrators of violence and alcohol addicts, while men were viewed as responsible breadwinners and loving fathers. No one says that such cases are impossible, but the way in which they are presented – as though violence perpetrated by women were as common as that carried out by men – is a deliberate distortion of social reality and is, in fact, aimed at marginalizing and neglecting gender-based violence. It has also become fashionable to present women as the leaders of violent gangs who somehow force their subordinate male gangsters to commit the most cruel crimes. The situation in Poland seems to be serious and cause for concern. I was astonished when a woman who had initiated a programme against domestic violence asked our Centre to organize training for them and wanted us to include violence against men in the programme. Another recent surprise concerns the competition, announced by the local government in Warsaw, to run a shelter for victims of violence: the condition for NGOs which would like to run such a shelter was that it would be open for female and male victims of violence. This is alarming because it goes against all social reality in terms of the numbers of women in need of the safety and support available only from women-only environments. This recent development in Poland is certainly aimed at undermining the importance of male violence against women and women's human rights in general and, if continued, it will almost certainly induce long-lasting negative consequences for women.

Official Data and Their Limitations

It is difficult to estimate the actual number of incidents of domestic violence and other violent crimes against women. The system of collecting official statistics concerning violence is not well developed, and research into the subject is so scarce that the results do not allow us to estimate the extent of the problem. According to the results of research conducted in 1993 and in 1996 by the Public Opinion Research Centre, out of a representative sample of 1087 adult women 18 per cent admitted to being victims of domestic violence; 9 per cent to being repeatedly battered by their husbands, and the other 9 per cent to being beaten sporadically during the relationship.

Responses changed as a result of divorce. Divorced women admitted abuse far more often: 41 per cent alleged that they had been repeatedly beaten by their husbands, and 21 per cent said that the abuse occurred

FIGURE 1

MARRIED WOMEN'S RESPONSES TO QUESTION: 'DOES OR HAS YOUR
HUSBAND EVER HIT YOU DURING A QUARREL?'

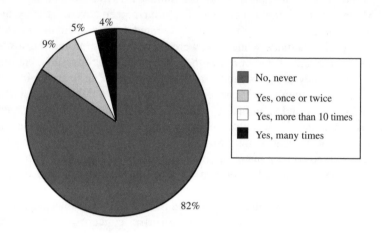

FIGURE 2

RESPONSES TO THE QUESTION:
'SOMETIMES IT HAPPENS THAT DURING MARITAL ARGUMENTS THE HUSBAND
BEATS HIS WIFE. HAVE YOU EVER WITNESSED OR KNOW OF WOMEN WHO ARE
BEATEN BY THEIR HUSBANDS DURING MARITAL ARGUMENTS?'

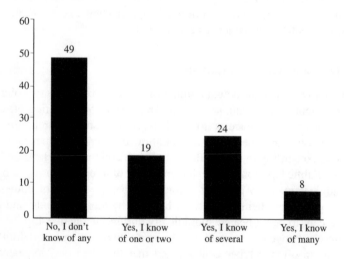

sporadically. Some women, however, keep the abuse secret. This is shown both by the data on the confirmed cases of abuses, and indirectly by the responses women gave to the question of whether they knew of any women who were beaten by their husbands during domestic conflicts. Of those women questioned, 41 per cent of married women and 61 per cent of divorced women answered 'yes'. Among the reasons given by the divorced women as to why they had divorced, 32 per cent of women cited physical abuse, while only 2 per cent of the divorced men offered the same response.

This means that almost half of the women in Poland personally know a woman who has been beaten by her husband. One in 20 Polish women lives in an abusive environment. However, it is difficult to be exact about what the indicators of an abusive environment are: wealth or poverty, high or low levels of education, many or no children, and so on. Most of the women polled responded that the abused women whom they know are from a wide socio-economic range. The women polled who knew the highest number of abused wives were mainly divorced or unemployed women. The women who noticed the most violence in their neighbourhoods came from small villages and large cities. The women who responded that they noticed violence in their neighbourhoods were mostly around age 24, or students; older women responded the least frequently. It is important to mention that these data concern only physical violence within marriage and do not cover psychological and sexual abuse in non-marital relationships.

The research also shows that domestic violence occurs more frequently in families living in rural villages and happens more frequently in low-income families, while education level appears to have no impact on abusive behaviour. The main and most available source of information about cases involving domestic and other forms of violence is the data published by the Ministry of Justice regarding sentencing. The court statistics show that in 1996, 15,412 domestic violence cases went to the court but only 12,087 resulted in a sentence. According to the data, the number of convictions for domestic violence crimes has increased over the past few years from 10,449 in 1993 to 13,405 in 1996. The number of suspended sentences also increased from 9,143 (87.5 per cent) in 1993 to 12,087 (90.1 per cent) in 1996. The rate of recidivism is very high (72.4 per cent), which indicates that the punishments for these crimes are not effective. More detailed statistics are available in the report.

The Ministry of Justice statistics indicate that 98 per cent of the perpetrators of domestic violence are men. In addition, the results of a study (conducted by Professor Kołakowskiej-Przełomiec) indicated that 81 per cent of the victims are the perpetrator's wives; eight per cent are their mothers; five per cent are their former wives, three per cent their live in partners, one per cent their children; and two per cent their parents-in-law.

The Ministry of Justice also reported that women are the perpetrators in only 1.5–2 per cent of the total cases of domestic violence. The majority of these cases were child abuse, and not spousal abuse. It is clear from these numbers that men are overwhelmingly represented in spousal abuse cases. Unfortunately, the only data collected relate to the sentencing of perpetrators, and not to the characteristics of the victims.

Approximately 50 abused women per year attempt suicide according to the Ministry of Justice. Two hundred murder cases per year can be traced to a family dispute. In 1996 there were 15,412 reported cases of family abuse falling under Article 184. Among these cases, 13,405 resulted in some form of sentencing. While 12,087 were sentenced to gaol, none of these people actually served time. Instead, they received probation or release conditional on fulfilling certain requirements set by the court, such as community service or remaining free from further criminal incident for a period of time. There are some other sources of official data on domestic violence in Poland. The police are required to keep records of the number of domestic violence cases sent to the prosecutor, but because of the lack of a computerized system for collecting data, the cases are not well processed and accurate data are difficult to obtain. The police are not required, however, to keep records by category of the offence of every phone call and resulting intervention. The data do not indicate the number of cases where charges were withdrawn by frightened women who had been seriously beaten or threatened with greater violence if they pressed forward with the charge.

Existing Law and Practices

Domestic violence: The Penal Code in Poland contains a specific provision which identifies an act of domestic violence as a criminal offence. It was introduced to the criminal code in 1969. Crimes of abuse against family members are found in the Criminal Code Chapter entitled 'Crimes Against Family, Custody, and Juveniles'. This provision covers both physical and psychological violence and is gender neutral. Art. 184:1 states: 'Anyone who abuses physically or psychologically a member of a family, an intimate relation, a physically or mentally disabled person, or a juvenile may be found guilty and sentenced from six months to five years in jail.' The perpetrator may be gaoled for up to ten years in the case of attempted suicide by the victim as a result of the abuse, or if the perpetrator acted with extreme cruelty (Art.184:2).

Under the new Criminal Code, enacted on 1 September 1998, the description of Article 207 abuse is the same. The minimum sentence for this crime was lowered from six months to three months. Under 207:2, if the perpetrator acts with unnecessary cruelty, the punishment is from one to ten years; if the victim attempts suicide because of the abuse, the punishment is from two to twelve years.

The law does not require the perpetrator to commit both physical and psychological harm to be found guilty under this provision: committing one type of violence is sufficient. In practice, though, most cases present circumstances in which both physical and psychological harm are present.

Definitions: 'Abuse' constitutes behaviour intended to cause either physical or mental (emotional) harm to another person. 'Physical abuse' can be defined as, among other things, punching, kicking, slapping, stabbing, or grabbing another person with the intent to hurt them. 'Mental abuse' may be defined as threats, insults, and words that degrade and humiliate, and that are intended to create low self-esteem and a sense of worthlessness in another person. An 'intimate relation' is a person with whom the perpetrator is either materially or emotionally connected in some way. An example of an 'intimate relationship' is a man and woman who share a home and raise a family together, but never get married. Another example is a couple which is divorced, yet continues to share a home, takes joint responsibility for raising their children, and continues to live as married people even though legally they are divorced.While the definitions in the law provide a starting point for judicial interpretation, it is imperative that judges interpret these definitions broadly, and evaluate the circumstances of each case individually in order to reach a fair result.

Domestic violence is publicly prosecuted in Poland and there is a legal obligation for the police and/or prosecutor to start an investigation when they find it is likely that domestic violence was committed. There is no need for the victim to come forward with the charges. It should be enough that a neighbour or NGO inform the police or a police officer observes acts of violence during a call to an incident. But 'the letter of the law' and the 'law in practice' are often two different things. In fact, cases of domestic violence are rarely treated seriously either by law enforcement or by prosecutors. In common practice, these cases are prosecuted only at the request of the victim. Additionally, police and prosecutors require well-documented complaints by the victim, and refuse to proceed otherwise. Often investigations of cases reported by women are not initiated because the evidence is not considered 'credible' by police or prosecution standards. The police require numerous medical certificates, which women have to get themselves and have to pay for, and numerous visits to the police station. While the public health service in Poland is free, a medical examination which will stand up in court must be paid for, and this fee is often unaffordable for many women (more than US$10 per certificate). The other reason for the lack of medical certificates required by the police is the fact that women are ashamed of their injuries. They do not seek medical attention because of the social stigma attached to battered women as well as their fear that they will be abused again. Although it is a possible for the medical examination to be free if women are referred by the police or prosecutor, this rarely happens and women are not informed of the possibilities.

Because domestic violence is a crime which occurs repeatedly, the seven-day rule also causes problems for women. If a woman has only one medical certificate indicating that the bodily harm she experienced is below seven days and she has no witnesses, the police may refuse to prosecute the case and inform her that she may file a private charge against her husband. The other problem victims of violence experience is the lack of witnesses. Neighbours are often unwilling to get involved, and do not want to be witnesses because they feel domestic abuse crimes are a private matter to be settled within the family. As a result they often refuse to testify. Police and prosecutors who are unwilling to develop a case against the perpetrator usually base their decision on the lack of evidence. It is a common notion in Poland that evidence of domestic violence is difficult to obtain, and therefore cases are difficult to prove. It is, however, also true that the police do not take an active role in gathering evidence, for example, by questioning neighbours immediately after an incident, when they may be more willing to testify, or by collecting and documenting other evidence at the scene.

When the police do decide to start an investigation the whole process usually takes several months. In the meantime, the victim goes through a process which is intimidating, unfamiliar and unfriendly. She cannot obtain adequate legal protection and is exposed to the perpetrator's revenge. Protection orders are not available in Poland, and there are very few shelters where victims can find refuge. As a result, the frightened victims often do not want to testify, refuse co-operation with the police and withdraw their complaints. Witnesses are often similarly frightened and are also exposed to the perpetrator's threats of revenge, and, as a result, pretend not to have heard anything or openly refuse to testify.

Because family violence cases are considered insignificant they are not treated like other crimes by the criminal justice system. One reason for the serious underenforcement of the existing domestic violence law is the absence of public recognition of the grave consequences for women who are the targets of violence and for children who are the witnesses of violence. There is virtually no public pressure to change this drastic situation. In fact, it seems that domestic violence in many communities is still accepted as an almost inevitable part of daily life.

Serious legal and institutional deficiencies in the family violence intervention system are also caused by a lack of knowledge about the complexities of domestic violence among policemen, prosecutors and judges. The result, therefore, is unresponsiveness to the injuries of battered women and their children, and the handling of their cases in an insensitive and ineffective manner. Many law enforcement officers and judges fail to apply the existing law effectively and often make rulings based on stereotypical attitudes and beliefs. This results in many victims not receiving the protection they are entitled to under the law.

The approach of the criminal justice system to the domestic violence cases is best reflected in the statistics. Suspended sentences are prevalent and their frequency has increased from 9,143 (87.5 per cent) in 1993 to 12,087 (90.1 per cent) in 1996. The fact that most perpetrators are sentenced to probation and not gaol is not surprising, since in 1976 the Highest Court issued guidelines that the lower court's first priority in these cases should be to keep the family together, and only in the most extreme circumstances should the perpetrators be sent to jail. Because there are no behaviour modification or rehabilitation programmes for abusive men in Poland, this ruling may in fact be causing more harm then good. Suspended sentences in practice are often no punishment at all. Offenders with suspended sentences often continue their criminal activity but very rarely are put in prison. Imprisonment is mandatory only after the second conviction, and because of the slow pace of the criminal justice system in Poland, it is unusual to be sentenced to mandatory imprisonment. The recidivism rate for Article 184 crimes is 72.4 per cent, which indicates that the punishments for these crimes are not effective.

TABLE 1

SENTENCING UNDER ART. 184 §1

	1993	1994	1995	1996
Total convictions	10,449 (100%)	10,696 (100%)	12,594 (100%)	13,405 (100%)
Jail Actually Served	1,181 (11.3%)	1,228 (11.2%)	1,272 (10.1%)	1,047 (7.8%)
Probation (suspended sentence)	9,143 (87.5%)	9,601 (87.6%)	11,183 (88.8%)	12,087 (90.1%)
Total Jail and Probation	10,324 (98.8%)	10,837 (98.8%)	12,455 (98.9%)	13,134 (98%)
Limited Freedom	63 (0.6%)	66 (0.6%)	63 (0.5%)	110 (0.8%)
Fine	63 (0.6%)	66 (0.6%)	63 (0.5%)	161 (1.2%)

Although there is a noticeable increase in the number of convictions, one must be careful when interpreting these data. It is obvious that social and political changes of recent years and women's increased awareness of their rights are factors in the rise of both of reports of domestic violence and convictions. However, many cases of domestic violence never get reported.

The following table shows the length of sentences and also reflects the attitude of the criminal justice system to domestic violence.

TABLE 2

THE LENGTH OF SENTENCE FOR CONVICTIONS BASED ON
ART. 184 §1 OF THE CRIMINAL CODE

	1993	1994	1995	1996
Below 6 months	0.5%	0.4%	0.5%	0.6%
6 months to 1 year	72.9%	75.9%	76.8%	76.5%
1 to 2 years	26.2%	23.2%	22.4%	22.5%
2 to 5 years	0.4%	0.5%	0.3%	0.3%
5 years	—	—	—	—

Despite the fact that according to the law a perpetrator of domestic violence may face up to five years' imprisonment, in fact more than 90 per cent get a suspended sentence and a maximum up to one year (77.1 per cent). The perpetrators are aware that they will most likely receive the lowest possible punishment for their crimes, and often feel they are immune from punishment altogether. As a result, the family physically remains intact and the short, suspended sentences contribute to increased tension resulting in further violence.

The unresponsiveness and ineffectiveness of the criminal justice system in the case of domestic violence means that many women never report the violence they have experienced. Those who do so often retract their statements later. The fact that Poland is experiencing a housing shortage also contributes to women's reluctance to report violence. The few houses for homeless people, where women may be exposed to further victimization, do not provide a solution in the long run, and many women often end up returning to the home they share with the abuser. Most abusers merely receive probation and return home after being sentenced, and women are fearful that, if they pursue a case against their partner, they will only be beaten worse the next time.

Rape: According to Polish law, rape is a crime against personal freedom and is gender neutral. It is a publicly prosecuted crime but the request of the woman is needed to start a prosecution. Article 168, §1 of the Penal Code defines rape and the penalty for the perpetrators in the following way: 'Anyone who by means of unlawful threat or deceit forces a lewd act on another person is liable to penalty of 1 to 10 years.' Article 168:2 states that if the offender commits the crime with unnecessary cruelty, or commits the crime with other people, the gaol sentence cannot be lower than three years.

Marital rape and homosexual rape are covered by the general provision. The definition of rape seems to be very modern and liberal. It includes the following elements: a violent act with sexual intentions in which the attacker uses physical force, threats, and/or coercion to overcome the victim's will and resistance when the victim has not consented to the act, and when the victim believes at the time of the act that she is being raped. An actual completed act of sexual intercourse and penetration are not necessary for a person to be found guilty of rape under Article 168. Any act intended to satisfy some sexual needs in the attacker is sufficient.

The Criminal Code does not explain the term 'unnecessary cruelty', but based on the guidelines of the Highest Court, this term means behaviour that is not essential to overcome the resistance of the victim, or a kind of behaviour intended to humiliate the victim, or to make her feel physical or moral pain or suffering, or to cause serious injuries or disfigurement to the victim. Under the new Criminal Code effective from 1 September 1998, rape is included under the section 'Crimes Against Sexual Freedom and Morality' and is defined as follows:

> Article 197 1: Anyone who uses physical force, threats, or coercion to force another person to engage in sexual intercourse against their will may be sentenced to gaol from one year to ten years.

> Article 197 2: Acting with the same force, threats, or coercion described in 1 above, if the perpetrator forces a person to engage in some other sort of sexual activity, not necessarily sexual intercourse, he may be sentenced to gaol for three months to five years.

> Article 197 3: If the perpetrator commits a rape as described 1 and 2 above and acts with unnecessary cruelty, or commits the rape with the help of another person, he can be sentenced to gaol for two years to twelve years.

At the Women's Rights Centre we are critical of placing the rape provision in a new chapter. We question why there is a need to distinguish between personal freedom and sexual freedom and what is the difference? In addition, what does the word morality included in the title of the chapter mean? What is the relationship between individual rights and morality? These are complex questions which deserve full consideration.

In practice, the execution of the law diverges from its letter. The police and courts treat rape as an everyday incident resulting from the provocative behaviour of women. The preparatory and judicial proceedings are gender biased and women victims are repeatedly treated as if they were the accused. Often rape victims are still in shock when they report the crime to the police, and it is not uncommon for the victim to be interviewed for hours at the police station. The police often treat the victim as a 'whore', as if she deserved to be raped. She is commonly humiliated for what has happened to her, and sometimes forced to confront the attacker at the police station. These facts cause additional psychological and physical harm to the victim, and she is often unwilling to identify the attacker for fear that he will retaliate against her or her family.

Despite the fact that as early as 1972, and again in 1979, the Supreme Court issued instructions to the lower courts that the law should be applied in accordance with its letter, judges admit evidence which, according to the regulations in force, should not be taken into consideration. During the trial the attention of the court is focused on the woman, who must prove that there was nothing in her behaviour that might have provoked the rape. The behaviour and lifestyle of the victim are under scrutiny and play an important role in sentencing. The fact that the request of the woman is needed to start the procedure seems to be a weak point in the law. Many women do not press charges due to their fear of the perpetrator's revenge, because of the humiliating investigative procedure or simply because they do not believe in the effectiveness of the criminal justice system.

What can be learned from practice is that the victim's sexual life prior to the rape will be taken into account by the court. It is generally accepted by legal scholars in Poland, and by the courts, that if the victim was passive or attempted to negotiate with her attacker, she did, in fact, consent to the crime. In these cases, the court evaluates the circumstances surrounding the rape with a more sceptical view of the victim, and is more likely to impose a lighter sentence on the attacker because of the victim's supposed consent. In determining guilt and severity of punishment, the court also takes into consideration how the woman was dressed or whether she behaved 'provocatively' (by coming to the house of the perpetrator) or if she was intoxicated. Usually the court will also take into account whether the woman was a virgin or not, whether the victim and the attacker knew each other, and whether they have had sexual relations in the past. All kinds of stereotypes come into play.

Although there are no accurate data in Poland we can assume that, as in other countries, the majority of rape cases occur in a situation when the attacker and the victim know each other. It is difficult to prove acquaintance rape since the attacker will often defend himself by saying that the sex was consensual, or that she enjoyed the brutal sex based on his previous relationship with the victim. There is some indication that the situation is improving in that the media have recently reported that a prosecutor has filed charges against a man who raped a prostitute.

Cases of rape and enforced sexual intercourse occur fairly often in marriages. Prior to 1990, convictions for marital rape were unusual and although women have become more aware of their rights over the last few years, they still do not report such incidents as crimes. They are ashamed of their situation and afraid of public opinion. Many women believe that being married means allowing a man to have access to their body at any time. Apart from that, they know very well that to prove a rape in marriage is not an easy task and the husband may always say that the sex was consensual. The only witnesses of the rape may be the children and most of women, as in cases of domestic violence, do not want to get children involved. If a woman decides to report violence it is usually in the context of domestic violence and even when she mentions forced sex policemen usually ignore it. It is a common tendency to put all kinds of violence, including rape in the family, as domestic violence to diminish the responsibility of the perpetrator since the sentence for rape is much higher than for domestic violence. Even attempted murder was classified by the prosecutor as a crime of domestic violence in the case of one of our clients.

Women who have survived rape have difficulties in finding specialized psychological assistance and counselling. There are practically no rape crisis centres in Poland and very few professional psychologists who may adequately address the specific problems victims of rape are facing. Under Polish law, the victim must report the rape before the police will start an investigation. Even if there is a witness to the rape who reports the crime to the police, the police cannot begin an investigation until the victim herself has filed charges. This procedure makes victims vulnerable to the perpetrator's insistence that the victim withdraw charges. Rape cases often take a long time and women are often victimized during the whole process, and their credibility is questioned. It is often difficult to prove because there are rarely witnesses to the crime and according to the rules of criminal law, the defendant is given the benefit of the doubt. If there are weaknesses in the victim's case, the court will weigh the evidence in favour of the defendant.

Taking into consideration the hostile attitude of the criminal justice system to victims of rape and the fear, guilt and shame, imprinted in women's minds by traditional stereotypes and the biased culture, it is easy to understand why cases of rape are so underreported. There are no accurate data in Poland but it is estimated that the number of rapes is actually ten times higher than what is noted by the police. There are also no data available on the number of cases reported to the police. The only available statistics concern sentencing.

Despite the fact that the law considers rape to be a serious crime, sentencing does not reflect the approach of the legislator. Only 64.2 per cent of rapists serve a gaol sentence.

TABLE 3

SENTENCES UNDER ART. 168 § 1

	1993	1994	1995	1996
Total	769	723	768	776
	(100%)	(100%)	(100%)	(100%)
Jail	525	482,3	493,8	498,2
	(68.3%)	(66.7%)	(64.3%)	(64.2%)
Probation (suspended	244	240,7	274,1	277
sentence)	(31.7%)	(33.3%)	(35.7%)	(35.7%)
Total Jail	769	723	768	775,2
Sentences	(100%)	(100%)	(100%)	(99.9%)
Loss of Civil and Public	19	—	—	—
Rights	(2.5%)			
Limited Freedom	—	—	—	0.78
				(0.1%)

The length of sentences also reflects the attitude of judges to rape cases: nearly 19 per cent of rapists got a sentence below the minimum stipulated in the criminal code, and 54.2 per cent received the minimum sentence of up to two years, mostly suspended.

TABLE 4

LENGTH OF SENTENCES UNDER ART. 168 §1

	1994	1995	1996
6 months to 1 year	158.3	152.8	145.9
	(21.9%)	(19.9%)	(18.8%)
1 – 2 years	342.7	410.8	420.6
	(47.4%)	(53.5%)	(54.2%)
2 – 5 years	188	166.7	176.1
	(26%)	(21.7%)	(22.7%)
5 years	22	16.1	13.9
	(3%)	(2.1%)	(1.8%)
more than 5 years	12.3	20.7	17.8
	(1.7%)	(2.7%)	(2.3%)

Prostitution: Prostitution is not a criminal offence in Poland. Under the Criminal Code it is a crime only when person gains money or other benefits from somebody else's prostitution or forces a woman to prostitute herself. The law reads as follows:

> Article 174 1: Whoever forces another person to be a prostitute may be sentenced to gaol for a term of one to ten years.

> Article 2: Whoever obtains material benefits from a prostitute's activities, or who enables the prostitute's activities, may be sentenced to a term of one to ten years in gaol.

Under 2, a person may be convicted for 'pimping' if they arrange the prostitute's contacts or earn a portion of money obtained in return. Pimping activities include, for example, borrowing or renting an apartment for the prostitute's activities, introducing clients to the prostitute, and arranging for the contact.

In Poland there is a common practice of prostitutes or pimps advertising services by placing small leaflets on car windshields or in hotel rooms. Also, a person may be found guilty under the Article 174 if he or she owns and operates a house of prostitution. Today, there are people in Poland who want to abolish the 'enabling' provision of Article 174 because they feel the punishment is not a deterrent or helping to decrease the rate of prostitution-related crimes. In addition to the possible gaol sentence of 2, the court can also impose a fine on the perpetrator.

Although pimping and forcing another person to become a prostitute is a crime, the law is not respected in practice. For example, brothels are often disguised as massage parlours, and there are many advertisements in the newspapers for prostitutes. The criminal justice system and police do not respond at all to prostitution-related crimes, often completely ignoring the obvious indicators of pimping and forced prostitution.

Although it is against the law, even hard core pornographic magazines are publicly displayed and one can buy them in many newspaper kiosks. Pornographic shops are everywhere, including in the most busy shopping areas. There have been several actions organized by religious groups against public exposure and the selling of pornographic magazines as well as against sex shops. The organizers used the fact that the existing law in Poland prohibits distribution of pornography. These actions were well organized. They succeeded in frightening many kiosk owners and salespeople, and as a result they stopped selling pornographic magazines.

Prostitutes in Poland work under various conditions: some work from home, others in hotels or on the streets. There are several streets in central Warsaw where prostitutes are regularly found. It is also common for women to work on highway exits and along large roads, on parking lots and in restaurants. There are many foreign women who work as prostitutes, especially from the former socialist countries. In the western part of Poland, there is a big problem with young people going to Berlin for a weekend of prostitution. According to one newspaper report, many schools near the German border have a high rate of absentees on Friday because of these weekend trips.

Trafficking in women: The legal regulations regarding trafficking in women are found in the Criminal Code Introduction, Article IX 1 and 2. Section 1 reads that 'anyone who abducts, delivers, or entices another person in order to force them into prostitution, even if the person consents to the prostitution, may be sentenced to gaol for not less then three years'; 2 states that 'anyone who trafficks women, even if the woman consents, or children, may be sentenced to not less than three years'.

Under Section 1, the term 'entices' describes actions by one person who coerces or tricks another person into, for example, moving to a new town, giving up their passport or other important documents, or promising legitimate employment, and then forces the person into prostitution. The term 'abduct' means taking a person to a place against their will. Under Polish law, these two terms are used interchangeably. Even if the person drawn into prostitution agrees to be a prostitute, the person who abducts her may still be found guilty under this Article. Under Article IX, it does not matter if this person was a prostitute previously.

Organized crime groups play a large role in enticing and abducting women, and there are many methods for exporting prostitutes to Western Europe. Data on this crime are not clear because it is difficult to catch and prosecute those responsible for abducting women, but it is common knowledge in Poland that this crime is widespread. It is difficult to detect trafficking in women; although law enforcement agencies across many countries are attempting to co-operate, more co-operative efforts are needed to stop this crime.

This crime is also difficult to stop because women who have been forced into prostitution are often unwilling to speak about the crime upon their return home since they are frightened and are afraid of revenge. The women also try to forget what has happened to them and to start a new life, and worry that if they do speak out about the crime, they will be marginalized by society and unable to live a normal life. Today, there are very few cases in Poland that have been prosecuted under Article IX, and therefore data regarding this law are difficult to obtain.

Since 1995 there has been an NGO called La Strada to work exclusively on the issue of trafficking. La Strada co-operates with Interpol, an international police force, and with similar organizations abroad to combat trafficking in women. They run a hotline, try to monitor investigations and assist individual women. The organization is also trying to educate the public, especially young women, about the problem of trafficking. They are invited to schools, in particular near the border and in areas where many young women may be vulnerable to all kinds of propositions about easy money abroad. The problem of trafficking especially concerns regions in poorer parts of Poland and the region near the border with Germany.

Sexual harassment: The problem of sexual harassment in the workplace is a relatively new issue of public awareness and debate in Poland. A public opinion poll in September 1996 indicated that only four to six per cent of women said they had been sexually harassed at work. The situation in Poland is certainly not as good as this and these optimistic results do not reflect the real number of sexual harassment incidents in Poland. It rather indicates the low level of social awareness of what constitutes sexual harassment. The work of the WRC and our first successful case has significantly contributed to increasing social awareness of this problem. Over the last two years there have been many articles published on the issue, as well as many TV and radio programmes.

The law in Poland does not adequately address the issue of sexual harassment. In the Criminal Code article 170 (Art. 199 in the new code) can be used in more severe cases of sexual harassment. The language of the provision is as follows: 'Anyone who takes advantage of their power position in a relationship with the intent to gain sexual gratification may be sentenced to jail for a term of from six months to five years.' In the new criminal code the maximum sentence for that crime was decreased to three years.

Sexual harassment means that a person in a position of power holding some authority over the victim will cause the victim to suffer some adverse consequence if he or she does not submit to their sexual demands. According to the Supreme Court guidelines, this relationship can occur between employer and employee, supervisor and subordinate, and teacher and student. Taking advantage of a position of power may occur when a subordinate is required to follow the superior's orders, and the superior is aware that they are taking advantage of their position by demanding sexual favours unrelated in any way to their subordinate's employment.

This type of crime is investigated only if the victim reports it. Because of women's lack of awareness about the possibility of punishment for this kind of crime, difficulties in proving it, and unwillingness to speak about it for fear of losing their jobs, there have been very few cases brought to the courts. Ministry of Justice statistics do not even include this offence. Article 170 can be used only when sexual harassment occurs by a supervisor towards a person in a subordinate position. This article cannot be used when the sexual harassment occurs between people in the same power position in the workplace, because there is no subordinate relationship.

The amended Labour Code includes an article in the general provisions which imposes an obligation on the employer to respect the employee's dignity. This could be used to argue cases of sexual harassment. It has not been used yet and some lawyers argue that the general provisions are not the kind of rights which can be directly executed. At the Women's Rights Centre we are planning to test this article directly and are encouraging trade unions to get involved in this process. We have taken on several cases of sexual harassment at the Centre; one involved criminal charges. The first case was of a woman who worked for a United States company. We succeeded in negotiating a year's salary for her as a compensation for not going to court and leaving her job. This case was the first we used to publicize the issue of sexual harassment. We also succeeded in getting a woman reinstated in her factory after she was dismissed in retaliation for reporting incidents of sexual harassment.

There is also a possibility of using civil proceedings to gain compensation under the general legal provision of the protection of personal dignity. The work of the Women's Rights Centre has certainly contributed significantly over the past two years to public awareness about the issue of sexual harassment. We hope that it will translate into more court cases and legal and internal regulations providing better protection against sexual harassment.

The Women's Rights Centre's Work on Violence Against Women

The Women's Rights Centre is an organization working predominantly on violence against women, but we aim to see the issue within the broader context of gender equality and discrimination against women. Although violence against women is the main issue we are working on, we also work on cases involving gender equality in the labour market including, for example, sexual discrimination and reproductive rights. At the Women's Rights Centre we try to combine and balance legislative and policy aspects of women's human rights by providing legal counselling to individual women who are victims of violence and discrimination.

In providing legal assistance to individual women, the Centre focuses on counselling those women who cannot afford a lawyer or those whose cases seem to be so important that they could set legal precedents. Areas of our legal assistance cover mainly criminal law (domestic violence, rape, and sexual abuse of children) and family law (divorce, alimony, and child support), although we also cover property law and labour legislation. The assistance we provide women ranges from simple legal advice and writing legal papers, to assisting them in the police station, in the prosecutor's office, and in court, to testifying on behalf of our client or acting as an organization or person of trust in proceedings which are not open to the public.

We do not tell women what to do or pressure them to take a particular action. There is already enough pressure on our clients, and too many accusations that everything is their fault. What we do is listen to them, and explain what rights they have and how they can exercise these rights. If they decide to leave an abusive relationship, we support them and assist them in carrying out their decision. We inform women about their rights as victims and encourage them to act as an additional prosecutor. The opportunity to act as an additional prosecutor during the trial gives the victim the chance to take an active role in the process, and not just rely on the public prosecutor who may be insensitive to the issue of domestic violence and too overworked to be well prepared for the trial.

Monitoring the work of institutions applying the law is becoming an increasingly important function of the Centre. We are planning to establish a programme with a large number of law students who could go to the court, the police or prosecutors' offices with our clients. We think that it is very important to monitor the way the law is applied and to show the role of the existing gender bias and stereotypes in the court rooms, police stations and prosecutors' offices. We plan to use the new possibility of acting as an NGO in criminal cases more often, especially where we hope to set a precedent. Although the assistance we are providing for battered women is called 'legal', it is in fact much more than simply legal counselling. Unlike traditional lawyers, we listen to our clients and try to help them solve not only their legal problems, but other related problems as well. If women need specialized assistance we direct them to other institutions and organizations providing psychological and social support. Since February 1997 we have run a support group for battered women.

One of our activities at the Women's Rights Centre is publishing brochures and leaflets concerning women's rights. The Centre has published and distributed several publications such as: 'Learn your rights if you are a victim of violence' or 'How to leave an abusive relationship', as well as manuals on divorce and on women's rights in the labour market. We also published a series of leaflets on myths and facts about domestic violence, rape and sexual abuse of women and children. We distributed these materials to various institutions and organizations helping battered women. One of our main target institutions was the social welfare offices. By targeting social welfare offices, we succeeded in establishing good working relationships with some local social welfare centres. They advise some battered women to seek assistance with the WRC, and some of our clients are referred to the social welfare centres to receive help we are not able to provide. We also co-operate with an anti-alcoholism agency which has started an anti-violence programme that includes support groups for battered women and therapy for batterers. We have established contacts with local government authorities and we negotiate with them to receive sheltered housing for battered women. The Women's Rights Centre closely co-operates with an organization called the Women Against Violence Association run by women who have themselves been the victims of domestic violence.

Since its inception, the Centre has been assisting women who are victims of violence. As a result, we see very clearly the weaknesses of the existing criminal justice system and the urgent need for reform in each step of the intervention system. We perceive training and education for the key professions involved in the domestic violence intervention system as a crucial step in the reform process given the complexities of this problem.

Our focus is on three professions: policemen, prosecutors and judges. We believe that if efforts are concentrated in only one part of the system, for example in training police to be more responsive and to write up the charges for the violence, without making changes in the prosecutors' office or in the courts, then the system will be overloaded at one end and the same archaic practices which now prevent women from being served effectively will continue to operate.

In the spring of 1997 we started a series of seminars on domestic violence and gender issues for policemen and prosecutors to educate them about the problem of violence against women. The series of workshops is designed to recognize the issues and problems in the work of each profession dealing with domestic violence. We believe that for maximum effectiveness, training and education materials appropriate for each of these professions should be developed in co-operation with the professionals who will be using them. We invite international experts to each of these workshops and create a Task Force for each profession composed of selected individuals. The Task Force will review the workshop suggestions and develop training and educational materials on domestic violence in consultation with invited experts. These materials will be published by the WRC and will be made available free to members of each profession. One of the projects we are working on is concerned with legislation on domestic violence.

Concluding Remarks

If we compare the progressive language of international human rights documents with the actual improvement at the national level, we clearly see the large gap between verbal commitments and the reality. Fifty years after the adoption of the Universal Declaration of Human Rights and five years after the approval of the Declaration on Elimination of Violence Against Women, it is clear that violence against women still constitutes a challenge to the national and international community and to society at large. We need more than verbal commitments! We need political will and concrete remedies. We know what to do, we have to do it.

The government signed the Platform for Action and the Declaration on Elimination of Violence Against Women, and developed a good and comprehensive national plan of action: now we must finally implement it. In view of the legal and institutional reform aimed at establishing more effective systems protecting women against violence, the review of the existing national laws and comprehensive research are necessary in order to effectively combat violence against women. In the absence of accurate data, it is commonly assumed that violence against women and domestic violence are confined to 'pathological', alcoholic or impoverished circles. This assumption is further supported by the fact that the only governmental programme against domestic violence currently has been run by the agency working against alcoholism in Poland. It is inevitable that the connection between violence and alcoholism obscures or denies the existence of the power and control relationships between men and women – a well-documented research finding on domestic violence in other societies.

The year 1999 has been announced by the European Union as a Year on Violence Against Women, and all countries applying for membership of the EU have been strongly encouraged to join the activities planned for this year. It seems to be a perfect time for the Polish government to begin to undertake some activities in this field.

The 50th anniversary of the UDHR and the coming new millennium seem to be an appropriate time not only to celebrate our accomplishments but also to demand the quality shift in the approach to women's human rights and human rights in general. We must stress the positive obligation of governments to protect and promote human rights and demand that the international community and the institutions of civil society execute it. Governments must take the full responsibility for its commitments. We, as the representatives of civil society, must make governments accountable. We need, however, stronger mechanisms which will help to enforce government's commitments and obligations under international human rights law. We should call upon the international community to adopt, as soon as possible, the additional protocol to the Women's Convention and finally to adopt the Convention on Elimination of Violence Against Women before the year 2000.

In closing this article, allow me to use the words from the Women's Human Rights 1998 global campaign: 'Imagine a world where all women enjoy their human rights. Take action to make it happen.' We can do it!

Rethinking Citizenship: Analyses and Activism in Central and Eastern Europe

CHRIS CORRIN

Current debates concerning the intersections of citizenship and gender are considered by examining political engagements in analysis arising from particular citizens' interventions in Central and Eastern Europe (CEE).[1] In choosing to consider women's collective actions to resist violence (at home and in war) and to challenge anti-democratic policies, key aspects of state–society relations can be considered with regard to citizens' choices of gaining agency – in representation and resistance. Something can also be learned of how certain types of political engagement are excluded from political analyses of civic engagement by not being deemed 'political'[2] or outside the accepted discourse. Examples of active citizen participation across CEE countries assessed here include anti-war protests and the exclusion of women's voices in determining their life choices. Issues of resistance to ethnic, nationalist and religious fundamentalism are interwoven in many of these analyses. Within feminist considerations of citizenship issues of identity, migration and rethinking the values of citizen activity and analyses are apparent. Feminist campaigns and struggles to resist, aim to overcome and eliminate varying factors which combine to oppress women. The uniting of theory and action in practice is a key feminist objective. Women activists all over the globe have been united at the end of this century in both theoretical explorations and practical engagements concerned with women gaining full citizenship and human rights. The considerations here attempt to understand some of the reasons why this is so.

People on the Move

It is the case that during the last decade great movements of peoples have taken place within CEE. In his considerations regarding aspects of regime transition and population movements Claus Offe points out that

> Following the breakdown of the Communist regimes in Central East Europe all four of the ethno-territorial moves that were largely unknown in the other transitions dominate the scene: (1) erecting new borders through secession or demanding local and regional autonomy for minorities; (2) negating the legitimacy of existing borders; (3) moving people across borders ranging from 'voluntary' mass exodus to 'ethnic cleansing'; and (4) negating previously recognized ethnic differences through forced assimilation.[3]

Alongside these processes have developed new discourses regarding 'Non-Western Others'. The economic–political discourses have centred on notions of social cohesion and economic convergence while the cultural discourses focus on identity politics which construct ideas of 'Europeans' and 'Non-Europeans'. Within this, the specific definition of Yugoslavia as it was breaking up as being part of 'the Balkans', rather than South-Eastern Europe, resonates with images of 'Otherness'. This is clear with regard to ideas concerning 'European' values and to those proposed within the context of European Union citizenship expectations. Definitions of what it is to be a refugee have gained great political currency across 'Europe' and EU member states have constructed debates regarding 'economic refugees' (without asylum rights). Only those who cross country borders fleeing persecution based on specific factors are refugees; those who do not are 'displaced people'. Excluded from refugee status under the 1951 UN Refugee Convention are all who cannot prove that they face persecution as individuals as well as those fleeing economic conditions and political upheavals.[4] In such contexts official refugee status is vital for many to survive, yet the conditions within which such status can be gained are restrictive and exclusory.

The work of the *Centre for Women War Victims*[5] (Centar za žene žrtve rata) provides excellent examples of taking initiatives to be actively involved in designing and implementing projects which try to answer situations emerging from war and to move with people's lives. In considering the problems for refugees in the continuation of war, workers from the Centre began new project work immediately after the Croatian military actions in Western Slavonia in May 1995. Rada Boric explains that

> We began to work with the local population in the Pakrac area, finding women there fearful and traumatised. Croatian women were resentful of Serbian women. We started with individual counselling, then we formed self-help groups in women's houses ... Our intention is to help real and meaningful re-integration of both sides.[6]

Yet, Boric points out that, despite their respected work during these times, women were not able to have any participation in decision-making during the war years nor in the peace negotiations. Whenever women have undertaken pro-feminist actions they have been denounced as 'national traitors', 'witches' or 'lesbians'.[7] As Mica Mladineo Desnica asks: 'Why is the State so tolerant towards women's self-organizing in wartime while during peacetime it is seen as subversive activity?'[8] In this way a dualistic discourse is established in which 'good' women work in healing war wounds and rebuilding lost values in so far as they have the 'correct' values. On the other hand, 'bad' women attempt to voice political analyses with regard to their changing environment – in economic, social and political contexts – from perspectives of justice for all, accepting certain global moral parameters but not accepting narrow boundaries of hierarchical nationalist discourse. As such, civic actions by women's groups analysing the situation of refugees in their projects[9] are construed as being made by women outside the acceptable parameters of national(ist) and local politics. So, when those at the Centre demanded that the government reconsider the decision to abolish refugee status to 100,000 refugees from Bosnia (September 1995) as a direct violation of refugee human rights, the group was engaging in the type of civic dialogue which is accepted, if not heeded, in most democratic countries. In Croatia, during and following the war, the exclusion of assertive, autonomous and articulate women's voices raised to challenge authoritarian and anti-democratic policy decisions has remained a key means of stifling political opposition and denying certain individuals and groups their full citizenship.

In the refugee populations from Bosnia-Herzegovina and Croatia the vast majority were women and children, yet women's voices were silenced at all levels of decision-making with regard to war and to negotiating peace.[10] Despite women's activism at the forefront of much anti-militarist activity – public awareness campaigns against violence in war and at home, and peace actions which included aiding men who deserted from their national armies – their exclusion in the aftermath of conflict ranges from barriers to women's involvement with official peace negotiations, as peacekeeping monitors and in war crimes tribunals (except giving testimony) and from the higher levels of decision-making with regard to humanitarian aid and policies with regard to the return and resettlement of refugees.

'Other' Identities

As much feminist analysis highlights, issues of citizenship have been gendered from ancient times[11] with women excluded as 'incomplete men' or as 'Other'. In a recent collection on *Women, Mobility and Citizenship in Europe* the continuing importance of such reasoning in defining boundaries was made clear: 'The construction of identity and citizenship is based on differentiation from the "Other". To define identity is to define alterity, to define citizenship is the define boundaries of exclusion/inclusion'.[12] It is in this realm of the differentiated 'Other' that many women and women's groups identify their exclusions and work towards revising the political parameters within which they can include all aspects of themselves in their analyses and actions. In this way challenges are made to male-constructed notions of citizenship, and alternative means of integration and civic activism are presented.

In terms of the differential access to power involved in many locations of women's activism (from state and societal responses to changing political climates) clear voices are raised in acting to change unbalanced power relations which exclude women's voices from decision-making. A recent example of this was apparent in the Croatian feminist protests against the new draft of the abortion law in November 1998.[13] According to the NGO BaBe (Be active Be emancipated), a women's human rights group, two key issues are problematic: compulsory counselling and conscientious objection. In compulsory counselling there is room for intimidation, manipulation and coercion, and in a newspaper interview[14] Sanja Sarnavka argued that 'once again women are put into the position of adolescent, immature subjects that need guidance and control when making a decision about their lives and bodies'.[15] As to a gynaecologist's right to conscientious objection regarding abortion, there is evidence of hypocrisy whereby doctors object within the health service but will carry out abortions in private practice where money is involved. In turn, this makes abortion less accessible, affordable or acceptable. Challenges to the use of legislation curbing women's rights to bodily integrity and women's involvement in drafting such legislation have been apparent in many CEE countries since 1990.[16] This is a key area in which women's 'Otherness' of being able to conceive and give birth to children can be used to deny women's abilities to exercise their judgement on their life choices and thereby denying certain women full citizenship on the grounds of their gender.

Consideration of the complex of relations of power present in citizens' lived realities is central to much analysis of gender relations and democratic change and to strategies of resistance. Recognition of the importance of women's activism in politics, as citizens within hierarchical politicized frameworks, is highlighted by Biljana Kasić in her foreword to the collection *Women and the Politics of Peace*:

> The political, in the understanding of many of the presenters at the Forum, is expressed as a search for public responsibility for peace as an unquestionable value, an ethical imperative and the only alternative, and equally relevant to international makers of global politics of development as well as to local institutions of government, civil society and the population at large.[17]

Here Kasić is breaking down some of the binaries between state politics (at national and local levels) and those of citizens in society. Invoking the 'ethical imperative' is in the tradition of democratic oppositionists such as Konrad and Havel.[18] If political decision-making is not based on ethical principles recognized by all citizens then some safeguards are required for the protection of various interests. That peace activists form minorities in

times of war is not new, but when peace-makers involved in rebuilding civic
values and engaging in human re-integration are excluded through gender
discrimination, the anti-democratic and exclusive political climate is in need
of change.

Active Citizenship

Collections based on the experiences of women's resistance within war or
at times of catastrophe emphasize not only the various ways in which
women have actively and passively resisted, by taking part in political
protests and in creating various models of activism from local to
international, but also in the ways in which dialogues are generated and
critically applied.[19] In this work many women are actively recognizing the
'differentiated universalism' which Ruth Lister proposes. Lister argues for
a synthesis of rights and participatory approaches to citizenship which link
with notions of human agency. In such a theory the exclusory powers of
citizenship in relation to both nation-state 'outsiders' and 'insiders' are
recognized. In considering outsiders, it is proposed that 'a feminist theory
and politics of citizenship must embrace an internationalist agenda ... it
offers the concept of a "differentiated universalism" as an attempt to
reconcile the universalism which lies at the heart of citizenship demands of
a politics of difference'.[20] For groups such as the Centre for Women War
Victims in Zagreb these conceptions are given life by the ways in which
women work through the imposed and real differences among them towards
a holistic recognition of their means of resistance in an international
context.

Acknowledging women's differentiated positioning has been particularly apparent in the feminist analyses and activism within and across
the countries which had been involved in the Yugoslav wars. Examples of
active citizenship were apparent from the violence following the Bosnian
independence referendum in February 1992 to the recent peaceful political
protests by women in Kosova in 1998 and early 1999, against continuing
repression and oppression. The women's non-violent protests in Kosova
were indicative of the power of imagery in 'speaking' against violent
politics. The isolation of the people of Drenica was recognized as something
against which women in Kosova wished to act. On 8 March 1998
(International Women's Day) the Network of Women in Kosova mourned
the international silence in a series of protests. Their communiqué stated
that a march would take place on 16 March: 'Organized by the Network of
Women, women of Kosova carrying only bread under their arms for the
children and women of Dresnica shall march to Drenica in order to show
solidarity with children and women in curfew, surrounded by Serb police

and military forces' (Network communiqué, 8 March 1998). These women were making use of the most time-honoured means of protest – silent vigils and marches – and the most up-to-date technology via their international contacts of sending messages across the internet via e-mail to show that these atrocities were not going unchallenged and that international recognition and assistance was imperative.

While the focus here is on CEE countries it is clear that 'issues affecting women cannot be analysed in isolation from the national and international context of inequality'.[21] The international context is also one of cross-cultural activism which acknowledges varying dimensions to citizenship dilemmas. Given the gendered nature of the expression of violence, the legislation to protect women who are forced to move is uneven and inadequate, being non-existent, ill-framed or poorly executed. Migrant and refugee women's lack of citizenship status makes them vulnerable to many forms of exploitation and oppression. Feminist networks and campaigns have intervened in challenging the conditions which force women to move or do not allow them to remain, and have established information and support systems which attempt to alter the oppressive situations in which many women have to live. Feminist reworking of considerations surrounding citizenship aim for an inclusive synthesis which allows for women's agency while challenging structural constraints.

Engendering Citizenship

A major aim of feminist theorizing is analysing women's experience as a basis for political action, so revising the gendered nature of key political conceptions such as citizenship is a vital part of this process. In considerations of citizenship, the language of rights becomes important as this language can obscure the need for social and political change. In asserting legal rights, for example, it is clear that women's interests and experiences cannot easily be translated into the confines of rights discourse. This has been highlighted in considerations of legal mechnanisms dealing with male violence.[22] The need for a feminist articulation of human rights is powerfully argued by Charlotte Bunch, for moving beyond male-defined norms and existing gendered biases.[23] In this area much feminist networking and collective work is developing to challenge gendered notions of citizenship and support women's participation in effecting change.

General criticisms of rights language include the following: its individualism ignores 'the relational nature of social life'; it can make contingent social structures seem permanent, undermining possibilities for change; it consistently functions to protect the most privileged groups in society.[24] Feminist criticisms further propose that rights discourse oversimplifies complex power relations; official balancing of competing rights reduces women's power; and particular rights such as those of family or religion can justify women's oppression.[25] Several kinds of rights in the constitution of citizenship have been considered by theorists over time. T.H. Marshall[26] notes civil rights of citizens before the law, political rights of citizens for access to democratic means of exercising political power and social rights for all citizens to engage fully in social participation. These elements have been used both descriptively over time and as necessary preconditions for achieving full citizenship. Despite criticisms of this work, it has proved something of a basis from which many Western theorists have considered the concept of rights.[27]

In terms of 'European' development, citizenship rights in many West European countries developed in parallel with capitalism and its associated inequalities. In state-socialist societies in Central and Eastern Europe, civil rights were much reduced given the lack of private property and rights to free association, and political rights remained largely formal given the overarching power of the state organs. What remained were social rights in terms of access to material welfare on a low level.[28] Kim Scheppele notes that

> in contrast with the history in which people first claimed bodily security, property and contract, and later got the right to vote, and later still were guaranteed minimum subsistence, the trajectory in Eastern Europe has more nearly been the reverse. People are much more used to claiming the state has a duty to provide for material security than they are used to claiming the state has a duty to protect private property.[29]

It is clear that in the 1990s most countries in 'Europe' are undergoing what amounts to a crisis of citizenship. Certainly the balance which Marshall suggested between developing the economy and social rights is unbalanced in most countries (in favour of economic 'freedom') and the demands of globalization coupled with localism are being felt:

> The image of a weakened nation-state caught in a pincer movement between globalizing and localizing forces is a common refrain in the contemporary citizenship literature, although one should not exaggerate the demise of its power, not least its power still to exercise control over membership and citizenship.[30]

Feminist insights into citizenship highlight that the consistent exclusion of gendered realities is both historically contingent[31] and/or constitutive in the theory and practice of citizenship with women having roles as 'woman' in private and 'honorary men' in public life.[32] In arguing for a feminist synthesis Lister notes the importance of participation – citizenship as rights involving human agency which

> is particularly important in challenging the construction of women (and especially minority group women) as passive victims, while keeping sight of the discriminatory and oppressive male-dominated political, economic and social institutions which still deny them full citizenship.[33]

The distinction drawn between being a citizen and acting as a citizen is important in the context of feminist analyses and resistance to violence at all levels. Whilst many women remain subordinate in terms of hierarchical power relations, they nevertheless can and do choose to be agents for change, in their own lives and in those of other women. Working within feminist groups and campaigns, the actions of women can be seen as challenging the limited and restrictive gendered conceptions of citizenship. In the development of peaceful civic engagements challenging violence in war, Biljana Kasić shows the work of Stasa Zajović as highlighting the significance of women working across divisions in the Yugoslav war – that the *Women in Black*[34] (Žene u črnom) anti-war protests have:

> manifestly shown, from the very beginning, a determination not to break this symbolic, valuable, bodily solidarity communication among women. The bodily resistance to war is a ritual of disobedience which the Women in Black, like their namesakes all over the world, have consciously chosen. By exhibiting their bodies every Wednesday on the city square in Belgrade, at the same time they were building ' … networks of disobedience to all militarists: fathers of nations, … guardians of states and borders'.[35]

Here, the embodied reality of women's resistance to men's violence has been an explicit challenge to the militarist decision-makers in Belgrade and an important challenge to those within society who feel that there is nothing to be done in terms of resistance.

Perspectives on War and Peace

For those who viewed the cold war as involving a 'set of rules', so at its ending, certain peoples or countries were viewed as no longer following any rules. Media commentators throughout Western Europe and elsewhere presented the war in Yugoslavia as being concerned with 'ancient' or 'barbaric' beliefs or feuds. In this way the focus is centred on 'identity' as an explanation, so that structural inequalities are marginalized and structural violence is ignored. The peace 'settlement' brokered externally for those at war is a case in point. Groups from various 'sides' in the conflict have argued against the sense of injustice – about being put through this 'settlement'. Such issues as access to land and extreme inequality and poverty remain much the same after such 'settlements'. Given that women and children are the majority of those displaced, the 'settlement' has signally failed to address their needs. For a powerful insight into the ways in which women refugees[36] from Bosnia-Herzegovina and Croatia have spoken of their lives as refugees, the collection 'The Suitcase' is a memorable one.[37] Images of women come to the fore in crisis situations and media involvement is still a key issue for protesters. Women in Priština were contacted about the third peaceful protest of women in Kosovo in 1998 and were asked 'Will there be violence?'. Apparently if there is not to be any violence then the media are not interested in 'the story'. The images of refugees crossing the borders of Kosova into Albania and Macedonia in 1999 were powerful catalysts in motivating public opinion in Western countries towards giving aid. Public opinion remained divided on intervention by bombardment and many feminist groups had been arguing for negotiated political settlements for a considerable time.

It is apparent that dramatic changes, whether in the form of 'democratization' in Central and Eastern Europe, or in forced population transfers apparent in the wars in Yugoslavia, are not gender-neutral and women's lives are being crucially affected in many different ways. Much of the economic change across 'Europe' has had far-reaching negative consequences for particular groups of women, especially women from 'minority' communities, poor women and women migrants. Within conflict situations, different racialized and ethnicized 'national' political agendas are often projected in terms of 'cultural difference'. Many women, whether they would wish it or not, have no involvement in some of the new political structures. Poverty and insecurity around returning to their homelands, gaining citizenship or rights or employment (or all three) are increasing within a context of declining legal and social welfare supports. The social stratification and economic differentiation between individuals and groups of women appears to be ever increasing.

'Women's Issues' Under Militarism

Patriarchal systems are based on the use of power. Militarist systems are based on violence and its threat. In assessing various aspects for consideration, the intermeshing is clear in the systemic uses of power. Rada Ivekovic notes the concentration on notions of sexual difference in the language of war:

> The entire nationalistic, nationally-constructed, warrior's language is
> highly sexualized. The nation, homeland, 'pure race' are all

represented as a vulnerable female body, the foreign borders are the ones that have to be forced through, like other men's wives, and 'ethnic' cleansing is primarily sexual. This is about proving and achieving birth and origin from the same 'clean' principle, and not from a different one. An ideally pure and cleansed nation, as a caste or, after all, religion, is male and does not even include women, or it gathers them only conditionally and in another manner than it does men[38]

Hierarchical systems of control are generally based on strict military rules and values. Military values such as physcial strength, aggressiveness, persistance and insensitivity are 'prized' and men are trained and conditioned in these 'values'. Militarist values are of concern not only in political and security issues but as a major factor in economics, culture and people's everyday lives. Within situations in which social control mechanisms are sanctioned and used to dominate, subjugate and exploit women, male violence can be analysed in the context of oppression based on the threat-system of militarism.

Nationalism is concerned with changing conceptions of femininity and masculinity in everyday lives. As Lepa Mladenović and Divna Matijasević pointed out, within this militarization of relationships in Belgrade boys are often addressed as 'my general' or 'my soldier' while girls become silent witnesses to boys being given double value – as boys and as army officers.[39] The increasing violence brought home from the front also featured in daily life. Women working on the SOS hotline in Belgrade noted the increased incidence of rape, torture and robbery by soldiers who come back to their families. Mica Mladineo Desnica from Zagreb notes attitudes towards 'women's issues':

> Besides, domestic violence, which has always been considered a minor, women's problem (if a problem at all), today has become a woman's patriotic duty. Women are being constantly taught (through the mass media) to feel ashamed to think about such selfish problems when the Nation and our men ('fathers, husbands and sons') are bleeding on the battlefield.[40]

Clearly women raising their voices against male violence at home when the 'national interest' is at stake are viewed as unpatriotic. In this context, those in power generally propose it to be women's 'duty' to keep the peace at home (regardless of men's violence) and produce children to replace those lost in battle.

As it is often women who pass on their cultural histories and moral outlooks to children, in circumstances in which certain cultural histories and moral values are being denied or reviewed, it is women who are pressured to fit in with ideological shifts which carry a gendered text – explicitly or implicitly. In her work on *Patriarchy, Language and National Myth* Stasa Zajović speaks of the ways in which Serbian nationalists brought back to life a symbolic medieval figure – Mother Yugovich: 'the long suffering, brave, stoic mother of nine, offering her children up to death in the defence of the fatherland'.[41] Along with the cult of blood and soil came the cult of motherhood, with maternity being viewed as an obligation and women's fertility closely monitored and controlled. In such contexts 'moral health' of a particular type is also prized so that state policies do not merely fail recognize other patterns of life as equal – one-parent families, childless women, lesbian partnerships – but they are designed to eradicate them. The elements of control here could not be more apparent. Women are forced into violent situations (enforced abortions, enforced pregnancies, continued cohabitation with violent men or forced migration) by the implementation of government policies designed to meet the needs of hierarchical agendas, couched in terms of the 'national interest'. The situations of women being systematically raped in war in Bosnia-Herzegovina highlighted the implementation of such violent agendas. This violent exploitation of women by men within ethnicized and nationalist contexts raises many questions and complexities in terms of how re-created images of 'good' and 'bad' women, ownership and objectification of 'our' or 'other' women are being violently fostered within or forced on to collectivities and communities, or both.

Women's 'Roles' in War

Enormous difficulties are generated by political misrepresentations of women's 'roles' in war and in creating peace. These can be overcome only once their roots and propaganda mechanisms are recognized. In writing of the gendered lessons learned from the war in Chechnya, Marina Liborakina from Moscow cites the terrorism of female hostage taking: 'The terrorists in Pervomaisk consciously chose pregnant women in the hospital as hostages to display the power over "Russian enemies". As well as in former Yugoslavia, the female body became a battlefield.'[42] Just as official discourse drops 'women' as a category from discussion, so often an official 'women's discourse' drops Chechnya as a category out of debates on the status of women. While women activists in Russia had been able to integrate violence against women into the list of 'permitted problems', nothing was being said about war, women in Chechnya or refugees. While women were acknowleged leaders of peace activism, only their role of 'mothers' was 'legitimised enough to justify interfering in a war regarded as male business'.[43] For Liborakina the main lesson from her feminist resistance to war in Chechnya was about women's citizenship:

> The key lesson that I, as feminist, have learned from war in Chechnya is about women's citizenship. As citizens, we are responsible for how we are governed. The main issue is not to elect 'a good President' but to form a system of civic control over the power and to broaden citizens' participation in decision-making, especially in decision-making on crucial issues of security, peace and military. Women must be citizens. This is the only way to protect women's lives and dignity, and the lives of our children.[44]

This is the significant thread throughout women's active resistance to various aspects and levels of violence – economic, political, social, marital, in the home, neighbourhood, country and across states – the recognition of women's ability to act on their own and others' behalf, within all spheres of politics and society. Moving beyond this recognition in surmounting the barriers placed against women gaining active voices in the 'male business' of decision-making on issues of security has proved both a difficult and a dangerous path to tread.

Contradictions and Connections

The contradictions which develop for refugee women, in immigrant women's situations or who have become 'trafficked' or are living within violent household situations in times of war and 'domestic peace', are many-layered and complex. The connections remain apparent at different times, particularly for feminist activists whose overviews are concerned with human rights and capacities, in addition to articulating other forms of citizens' activism which reaches across generated gulfs supported by hierarchical militarist systems of logic and material control.

Two streams in debates on nationality and citizenship are between blood and ethnos or birth and residence.[45] As theorists of nationalism have consistently stated, one of the ways in which a new state identifies its difference from its neighbours is by the production of a specific set of cultural ideas.[46] Increasing ethnic nationalism and conflicts over recent decades are evidence that across 'Europe' racism and xenophobia are constantly developing, with their roots in patriarchal relations of power. The gendered nature of racism has long been apparent. Avtar Brah has emphasized that 'it is necessary to reiterate explicity that racism is always a gendered and sexualised phenomenon'.[47] Across 'Europe' many communities are suffering greatly from racism and racist violence, and with various changes in citizenship legislation, many people from Africa and

Asia who now live in any part of 'Europe' not only have fewer rights to protection in law but are differently placed in their access to power and to law enforcement and judicial systems. Across many countries Traveller and Roma peoples are marginalized, suffering racism from skinhead thugs, racist political parties and interventions by government authorities. The ethnic nationalist tensions which were fermented in war in Yugoslavia unleashed violence against women at all levels including systematic rape and femicide.[48]

Nationalist fundamentalist projects have generated such violence as 'ethnic cleansing' in which women's bodies and minds become the maps of war territories.[49] The rise of religious fundamentalism in Poland culminated in the March 1993 law on abortion which clearly attacked the rights of women to decide whether or not to give birth to a conceived child.[50] Some agencies organized trips to Western countries but the costs (economic and pyschological) remained high. As has been the case throughout time, poor women were being forced to induce miscarriages by using risky methods or by going to non-professional abortionists. Other consequences of the oppressive nature of religious political projects can be seen in the violent suppression of women's sexuality which is strictly controlled across the globe. Acknowledging women's active sexuality is something that fundamentalist political movements undertake in order to control (and oppress) women. The range of abuses that lesbians face includes 'torture, including rape and sexual abuse from government officials, arbitrary imprisonment, "disappearance" and extrajudicial execution'.[51] As with other areas in which women suffer male violence, the violence which lesbians experience often remains hidden. As Lepa Mladjenović illustrates in 'Dirty Streets', violence against lesbians in Belgrade became starkly contextualized: 'When a local gang in my neighbourhood beat me up because I am a lesbian one of them said "You are dirtying my street".'[52]

Citizens of the World?

International feminist campaigns and writings have made analyses of the use and abuse of power in gender oppression apparent.[53] When rape in war is carried out, the continuum of violence takes additional forms, and the means of analysis are complicated by ethnic nationalism and ethnic 'cleansing'. The patriarchal use of power in naming – a situation, a person or a group – as 'unclean' becomes fatal. Again, some children are more important, more 'clean', than others and rape can be concerned with defilement of enemy women, breaking up the social fabric of communities, 'shaming' men via their women (that is, about men's 'honour') and as a means of breeding the 'right' children (rape in marriage). Women become ethnicized as enemy Others, rapists as men representing their national interest. The confusion and complexities here are apparent, with ideas concerning women in war as symbols of the nation – as 'ideal patriotic mothers' or as 'enemy whores'. The 'dying out of the nation' takes on even more sinister connotations in wartime. Cynthia Enloe points out that 'It is precisely because sexuality, reproduction, and child-rearing acquire such strategic importance with the rise of nationalism that many nationalist men become aware of their need to exert control over the women.'[54]

While nationalist men wish to protect their national interest and ensure the 'survival' of their nations by breeding the 'right' children, questions are raised about raping Other women in camps. The complexities of rape for impregnation confuse straightforward 'conceptions'. Do soldiers want Other women to bear their children? How will such mothers and children be able to live – together or apart – in what 'state'? Much information has been used for political propaganda, with the experiences of women survivors on all sides being 'used' to justify retaliatory violence and violations of human rights. As can be seen, manipulation of information for political aims leads to hatred, revenge and further violence.

That women make up the vast majority of internally displaced persons who are often unable to go 'home' leaves them vulnerable in the aftermath of ethnic conflict.[55] In terms of where 'home' is and where 'we' belong, Rada Boric sums how some feminists feel in terms of their place in the world:

> As women we are organizing because this is the only way to make our issues visible. We want to be activists, not passive victims. In all this nationalistic euphoria it is easy for me to choose my nationality: Woman. It is not enough to 'look at the world through women's eyes' (as the Beijing Women's Conference says). We must make the world a reflection of women's minds and women's efforts.[56]

It is in this area, of shared work commited to reflecting women's minds and efforts in feminist resistance to violence on all levels, that the dynamic enlargement of conceptions of active citizenship is being carried out. For example, it was recognized by women at the Helsinki Citizen's Assembly women's forum in Tuzla[57] that, in the aftermath of conflict, the 'settlements' generally failed to recognize, or wilfully ignored, women's needs and rights, and women in Tuzla and elsewhere choose not allow these ommissions to go uncontested. Women from Kosova in troubled times are seeking to make their voices heard in terms of peace and social justice for all oppressed groups.[58] The range of work undertaken by feminist groups internationally shows the connections that feminist activists are willing to make in their work, highlighting links across the causes and the methods of regulation of violence at many levels.

Feminist Resistance in Deeds and Words

The global nature of problems concerning the trafficking in women and the violence done to women in the face of ethnic nationalism and racism can be comprehensively addressed only when the interconnections are borne in mind. As is apparent in trafficking in women, issues of racism, objectification of women, failures of legal and judicial systems to protect women's and children's interests and issues of poverty and inequality, all play a part in making up the systems of exploitation. While the scale of the problem of trafficking in women remains largely 'hidden' and under-reported, the measures suggested to combat such trafficking are often double-edged in terms of their consequences.[59] Often, in such situations women have little recourse to protective legislation and risk deportation if they seek intervention because they are being beaten or abused in other ways. Deporting trafficked women generally serves only to perpetuate or increase their problems and neither prevents nor curtails trafficking. Deportations of trafficked women also make prosecutions almost impossible.[60] It is also apparent that women are trafficked for military 'needs'. Instances of Ukrainian women being brought to Croatia for 'use' by UN soldiers were known among feminist groups working in this area. A recent Amnesty International appeal case noted that 'two Ukrainian women were terrorised and violently abused by Croatian soldiers who were trying to evict them from a flat in Zagreb on 21st July 1995 ... Police called to the scene did not protect the women from these abuses ... .'[61] Challenging such blatant instances of gendered violence is complex as the levels of power use and abuse become more intermeshed at various levels. Certainly challenging the various 'European' mafias operating in trafficking in women demands particular care, in terms of self-preservation, on the part of women's groups and campaigns.

While poverty and the marginalization of women are root causes of trafficking, with measures to combat poverty and women's marginalization still very much needed, poverty alone does not explain the disparities between those who are trafficked. Women from some poor countries are more likely to be trafficked to Western Europe than women from other poor countries. There are clear racialized elements to much of this 'trade in women'. The racist elements of sexualizing Black women are ever-present.[62] The multinational aspect to trafficking, involving people from several 'European' countries, is such that operations can be moved at short notice. National legislation may just 'displace' the problem, either by changing immigration laws, which moves activities further 'underground', or by implementing restrictions which result in a shift of activities to another country.

Research is continuing at local and national levels by women's groups and organizations. In Poland the work of the NGOs Committee has highlighted the plight of many Polish women forced into prostitution by trafficking groups. A lack of information about women, often from Russia, who work in Polish sex clubs is noted in the report. The registration of prostitutes by police in Poland was ended in 1989 so that there are no official data from which to estimate the scale of the situation. It is in this context that the state interest is juxtaposed to that of social or feminist interest in certain women's situations:

> These spheres of social life seem to be beyond the state's scope of interest. Only women's and feminist organization recognize prostitution and trafficking in women as a problem and have undertaken activities aimed at forcing the Polish government to comply with the United Nations' provisions counteractiong violence against women.[63]

The recognition from women activists of the need for intervention against trafficking in women appears in stark contrast to state inaction on this global problem. The committee recommendations include (among others) the implementation of mechanisms safeguarding the execution of existing Polish regulations and international laws. Yet, as is often the case, generating the will to implement such laws with regard to women's safety generally requires changing social attitudes towards recognition of 'the problem'.

Conclusions

Feminist resistance to gender oppression and repression in war and domestic 'peace' through campaigns and networking with other groups highlights changing aspects of citizenship. The varying responses to conflict situations highlight many examples of analysis and resistance to the exploitation of women, and show the strength of women's collective energies in theoretical explorations and political resistance. This is certainly apparent in terms of active citizenship and the regeneration of civic resistance to hierarchical dictates. As Stasa Zajović expresses the position with regard to the six years of protest by Women in Black in Belgrade:

> Through testimony we want to leave a trace in people's consciences; we use non-violent methods to intervene directly in the reality in which we live; by assuming responsibility as individuals and as a small group, we speak in our own names, rejecting the patriarchal role of passive observers. With continuity we express women's

perseverance and resistance to war and a culture of death. By changing our relationship to ourselves, and through a different approach towards differences, relationships and conflicts, we achieve alternative politics.[64]

Here we see a crystal-clear vision of feminism in action in terms of both analysing what is happening within society and attempting to develop change that is positive for women, children and men.

As has been shown, feminist approaches are not unitary and do not offer simplistic solutions. Yet feminist considerations arising from our joint work can be a unifying force, encompassing ways in which women can fulfil their active participation in creating change in social and political domains. As Nira Yuval-Davis has pointed out, 'the most important duty of citizens is, therefore, to exercise their political rights in the determination of their collectivities', states' and societies' trajectories'.[65] As can be seen with feminist resistance against gender oppression, this struggle for citizenship does take place at the level of household and neighbourhood, within ethnic and national collectivities and in the international political arena. These activities form a basis for developing a foundation for millions of women in their struggles for change. From the work that many feminists are carrying out in difficult circumstances it is clear that, only by struggling on several fronts simultaneously and making links across various 'levels', can active citizenship aims be implemented.

NOTES

1. The term Central and Eastern Europe (CEE) refers to all of 'Europe' (currently the UN defines 55 countries) which is outside the area identified as 'Western'. Many newly independent states are included within CEE.
2. There are many considerations of what is deemed 'political' from a broader, alternative perspective. See initially C. Corrin, *Feminist Perspectives on Politics* (London: Longman, 1999).
3. See C. Offe, *Varieties of Transition: The East European and East German Experiences* (Cambridge: Polity Press, 1996), pp.31–2.
4. See J. Mertus *et al.*, *The Suitcase: Refugee Voices from Bosnia and Croatia* (Berkeley, CA: University of California Press, 1997), p.9.
5. When the mass rapes of women in Bosnia became known in 1992, feminist groups from Zagreb and Belgrade working with survivors of male violence began to organize to work on this. With the support of women's groups from around the world, centres based on feminist principles were opened in Zagreb, Zenica and Belgrade to work with women war survivors.
6. R. Boric, 'Croatia: Three Years After', in C. Corrin (ed.), *Women in a Violent World: Feminist Analyses and Resistance across 'Europe'* (Edinburgh: Edinburgh University Press, 1996), p.140.
7. Ibid.
8. M. Mladineo Desnica, 'Croatia: Three Years After', in Corrin (ed.), op. cit., p.134.
9. In early 1995 displaced persons and refugees made up 11.9 per cent of pre-war population in Croatia.

10. See Boric, op. cit., pp.135–52; Corrin (ed.) op. cit.; L. Mladjenovic, 'Dirty Streets', in Corrin (ed.), op. cit., pp.127–30; Mertus *et al.*, op. cit.

11. See V. Bryson, *Feminist Political Theory* (London: Macmillan, 1992); D. Coole, *Women in Political Theory* (Hemel Hempstead: Harvester–Wheatsheaf, 1994); Corrin (ed.), op. cit.

12. C. Corrin, 'Engendering Citizenship: Feminist Resistance to Male Violence in "Europe"', in V. Ferreira *et al.* (eds.), *Shifting Bonds, Shifting Bounds: Women, Mobility and Citizenship in Europe* (Oeiras, Portugal: Celta Editora 1998), pp.107–204.

13. The peace agreements in Bosnia-Herzegovina and Croatia resulted in new constitutions enclosed in the terms of the Washington Agreement and the Dayton Agreement. Among the Conventions that apply to the new constitutions is the Convention on the Elimination of All Discrimination Against Women.

14. The interview was with the newspaper *Slobodna Dalmacija* and another interview was given to the televion programme 'Latinica'.

15. See BABE, B.a.b.e. update, July–Dec. 1998, 6th issue, p.1.

16. World Health Organization Scientific Working Group on Reproductive Health Research 1999.

17. B. Kasić (ed.), *Women and the Politics of Peace: Contributions to a Culture of Women's Resistance* (Zagreb: Centre for Women's Studies, 1997), p.7.

18. Vaclav Havel, *The Power of the Powerless* (New York: Armonk, 1985); George Konrad *Anti-Politics: An Essay* (London: Quartet, 1984).

19. See Kasić, op. cit.; R. Lentin (ed.), *Gender and Catastrophe* (London: Zed Books, 1997); S. Zajović (ed.), *Women for Peace* (Belgrade: Women in Black, 1997).

20. R. Lister, 'Citizenship: Towards a Feminist Synthesis' (Citizenship: Pushing the Boundaries), *Feminist Review*, No.57 (1997), p.28.

21. A Brath, *Cartographies of Diaspora: Contesting Identities* (London and New York: Routledge, 1996), p.102.

22. J. Conors, 'Government Measures to Confront Violence Against Women', in M. Davies (ed.), *Women and Violence: Realities and Responses Worldwide* (London: Zed Books, 1974).

23. C. Bunch, 'Transforming Human Rights from a Feminist Perspective', in J. Peters and A. Wolper (eds.), *Women's Rights: International Feminist Perspectives* (London and New York: Routledge, 1995); C. Bunch, 'The Intolerable Status Quo: Violence against Women and Girls', in *The Progress of Nations* (New York: UNICEF, 1997).

24. H. Charlesworth, 'What are "Womens's International Rights"?' in R. Cook (ed.) *Human Rights of Women: National and International Perspective* (Philadelphia, PA: University of Pennsylvania Press), pp.60–61.

25. Ibid., p.61.

26. T.H. Marshall, 'Citizenship and Social Class', in T. Bottomore and T.H. Marshall, *Citizenship and Social Class* (London: Pluto Press, 1950; reprinted 1992).

27. See Chantal Mouffe (ed.), *Dimensions of Radical Democracy: Pluralism, Citizenship, Community* (London: Verso, 1992); Margaret Somers, 'Law, Community and Political Culture in the Transition to Democracy', *American Sociological Review*, No.58, pp.587–620.

28. J. Heinen, 'Public/Private: Gender, Social and Political Citizenship in Eastern Europe', paper presented at the Second ESA Conference, Budapest, Aug.–Sept., 1995.

29. K.L. Scheppele, 'Rethinking Group Rights', unpublished paper, 1994.

30. Lister, op. cit., p.37.

31. C. Pateman, *The Sexual Contract* (Cambridge: Polity Press, 1988); C. Pateman, *The Disorder of Women* (Cambridge: Polity Press, 1989).

32. J. Scott, 'Deconstructing Equality-versus-Difference: Or the Uses of Poststructralist Theory for Feminism', *Feminist Studies*, Vol.14, No.1 (1988), pp.33–50; K. Jones, 'Citizenship in a Woman-Friendly Polity', *Signs*, No.15 (1990), pp.781–812; N. Yuval-Davis *et al.*, 'The Potential Uses of Religion, Culture and Ethnicity: Cairo 1994', *Women Against Fundamentalism Journal*, No.7 (1995), p.13; J. True, 'Gendered Citizenship: "East–West" Comparison in a Post-War Era', paper at IPSA conference, Berlin, Sept. 1994; Heinen, op. cit.

34. *Women in Black* is a women's peace group which became active in Belgrade on 9 October 1991. It was modelled on the first group of Israeli Women in Black which began in Jerusalem in January 1988.

35. Kasić, op. cit., p.9; Zajović (ed.), op. cit., p.34.
36. The lay-person's usage of term refugee is used within 'The Suitcase' not the legal definition – all people who left their community and considered themselves refugees were eligible for the collection.
37. Mertus et al., op. cit.
38. R. Ivekovic, 'Women, Politics, Peace', in Kasić, op. cit., p.97.
39. Mladjenović, op. cit., p.122.
40. Mladineo Desnica, op. cit., p.136.
41. S. Zajovic, 'Patriarchy, Language and National Myth', Peace News, March 1992, p.7.
42. M. Liborakina, 'Women and Politics of Peace: Lessons Learned from the War in Chechnya', in Kasic, op. cit., p.125.
43. Ibid., p.125.
44. Ibid., p.130.
45. R. Kuma, 'Introduction', in R. Kumar and J. Kaldor-Robinson (eds.), National and Citizenship: A Discussion (Prague: Helsinki Citizens Assembly Publication Series 5, 1993).
46. E. Gellner, Encounters with Nationalism (Oxford: Blackwell, 1994).
47. Brah, op. cit., p.156.
48. Boric, op. cit.; Corrin (ed.), op. cit.; C. Enloe, The Morning After: Sexual Politics at the End of the Cold War (Berkeley, CA: University of California Press, 1993); Mladineo Desnica, op. cit.; Mladjenović, op. cit.; A. Stiglmayer, Mass Rape: The War Against Women in Bosnia-Herzegovina (Lincoln, NE: University of Nebraska Press, 1994).
49. H. Bresheeth and N. Yuval-Davis, The Gulf War and the New World Order (London: Zed Books, 1991); Enloe, op. cit.; Boric, 1996, op. cit.; Mladjenovic, op. cit.
50. On 24 October 1996 the Sejm voted a bill allowing abortion before the twelfth week if the woman has financial or personal problems.
51. Amnesty Report, 1995, p.11.
52. Mladjenović, op. cit., p.128.
53. S. Brownmiller, Against Our Will: Men, Women and Rape (Harmondsworth: Penguin, 1976); R.E. Hall, Ask Any Woman: A London Inquiry into Rape and Sexual Assault (Bristol: Falling Wall Press, 1985); A. Rich, 'Compulsory Heterosexuality and Lesbian Existence', Signs, Vol.5, No.4 (1980), pp.631–60; C. Smart, Feminism and the Power of Law (London: Routledge, 1989); Stiglmayer (ed.), op. cit.
54. Enloe, op. cit., p.238.
55. Mertus et al., op. cit.
56. R. Boric, 'The Oasis', New Internationalist (London), Aug. 1995, pp.12–13.
57. Two weeks before the ceasefire in Bosnia was brokered in October 1995, the Helsinki Citizens' Assembly held a large peace conference in Tuzla at which the Women's Commission conducted large seminars on topics from political fundamentalism to Yugoslav identities and women's voices for peace.
58. Women in Priština were on the streets in March 1998 taking part in non-violent resistance to the attacks, holding up blank pieces of paper to signify the lack of women's rights.
59. J. Conors, Violence Against Women in the Family (New York: United Nations Office, 1989); Corrin (ed.), op. cit.
60. It has been suggested that deportation is advantageous for some club owners, being a cheap way to send women home: see C. de Stoop, 'They are so Sweet, Sir', in International Organization for Migration, Trafficking and Prostitution: The Growing Exploitation of Migrant Women from Central and Eastern Europe (Budapest: Migration Information Programme, 1994).
61. Amnesty International, Appeal Cases, March–April 1988, p.7.
62. See International Organization for Migration (IOM), op. cit.
63. Polish Committee of NGOs, 'The Situation of Women in Poland: Report of the NGOs Committee', Warsaw, 1995, p.53.
64. S. Zajović (ed.), 1997, op. cit., p.1.
65. N. Yuval-Davis, 'Women, Citizenship and Difference' (Citizenship: Pushing the Boundaries), Feminist Review, No.57 (1997) pp.21–2.

Re-imaging Bulgarian Women: The Marxist Legacy and Women's Self-Identity

TATYANA KOTZEVA

In Bulgarian society under communist rule, two conflicting images of women were constructed: the socialist Amazon – a woman-android, the mechanical woman, woman-heroine of a socialist modernization project – and woman as a mother and carer of children. Recent investigation reveals a high degree of convergence in the self-identification strategies pursued by different groups of Bulgarian women, with some divergence among ethnic minorities. Despite general, abstract approval of gender equality and emancipation, women predominantly identify themselves with motherhood and caring within the family, and women's perceptions of self-esteem, sense of dignity, individual emancipation or unfair treatment are passed over in silence by significant numbers of women. A possible explanation for this is that in the situation of a radical reorganization of public institutions and blocking of women's access to influential public positions, family life becomes the only alternative space in which to invest personal energies.

This contribution focuses attention on the following questions: How can we understand what is going on in Eastern Europe in terms of gender? Who are these East European women whose 'otherness' creates a space for them to appear? Being stalked by the totalitarian past and trying to escape from it slowly or more quickly, do they become less different or do they remain trapped by an absolute of 'other time'? It is well known that gender is a political, cultural and epistemic category but it is at the same time a historical one, so we cannot 'read' the post-communist crisis using the language of gender without using all dimensions of this category. How could 'gender' unveil the case studies which have been labelled 'second' or 'fourth' world? And what do these cases mean when they have been discussed internationally? How do they influence the monolithic feminist discourse through their different cultural voicing?

Their cultural heterogeneity is a very important argument from which to conclude that there is no universal feminist voice or, as T. de Lauretis observes, 'the feminist subject ... becomes redefined as much less pure – and not unified or simply divided between positions of masculinity and femininity, but multiply organized across positionalities along several axes and across mutually contradictory discourses and practices'.[1] There are commonalities between the 'Second' and the 'Third World' which makes it possible for East European cases to be subsumed under studies of 'post-coloniality'. The paradigm of development and modernization for the post-communist societies and for the countries in the Third World prescribes for them the common status of marginality and opens space for 'their' 'minority' discourses. The claim that they reveal the authenticity of local and ethnic voices is proposed as a way of breaking the Eurocentrism of Western hegemonic thought and of avoiding the objectivism of non-Western realities. As H. Bhabha puts it: 'not only what is said but where it is said; not simply the logic of articulation but the topos of enunciation.'[2]

On the other hand, the category 'lived experience' is proposed as the only way to empower speechless minority voices with authenticity and the strength of the Truth. Unfortunately, the attempts of standpoint theorists to legitimize oppressive discourses frequently turn into a 'low-grade romanticism'[3] and confrontation of the main body of knowledge, expressed by the statement that understanding stems from living, not from studying. Thus, 'freezing people into the positions of authentic voice or deferential listener',[4] the position of 'lived experience' leads to an impossibility of dialogue and to a reinscription of a culture of monologue. Personal stories which are not told or read through the politics of dialogue between West and East could hardly make problematic the ethnicity and selfhood of 'native informants'.[5]

The only alternative to providing such a dialogue is to view identities always in change and transformation, or, as S. Hall puts it: ' ... actually identities are about questions of using the resources of history, language and culture in the process of becoming rather than being ... '.[6] Identity formation is a twofold process: on the one hand, to identify oneself means to take up positions which are imposed on the subject, whose representations are constituted through ideological mechanisms; on the other hand, identification means subjecting energy and investment to perform these positions. In these terms, identification is viewed as a 'point of suture' between the positions represented by the subjects and their contributions which are driven by both consciousness and the unconscious.[7]

Taking into account the ambivalent approach to identification – considered both as artificially enforced and as achieved 'selves' in the following pages – I discuss the construction of womanhood across different discourses and practices during the past five decades in Bulgaria. My first aim is to present socialist gender ideology as a mixture of two components: the 'populist–egalitarian' strand which emphasizes the equal involvement of men and women in paid work, and 'the "nationalist" strand that facilitates the idea of women's sense of loyalty and belongingness to state and nation'. Second, I try to elaborate how different discourses are being intertwined into women's self-conceptualizations during social transformation in Bulgaria after the collapse of the state socialism.

Women's Representations in the Marxist Discourse

Marxist ideology proclaimed its revolutionary effect, pretending to create an image of a New Woman. She was considered to be an icon of the prosperity and economic advancement of the newly-established system of socialism. The image of a socialist woman was elaborated to reinforce the unique mission of a woman to sacrifice herself in order to assist in the establishment and further development of the system towards a 'shining future'.

It is not surprising that the feminine vision of socialism is completely linked to the workplace and the public domain, owing to the mass mobilization of women in state-run factories (since the 1950s women have formed 50 per cent of the country's labour force). The visual rhetoric of socialism is imbued with photographs of women, looking proudly from the seat of a tractor, a conveyer belt or other technical appliance, which is emblematic of the socialist progressive transformations and the human race's domination over nature. The new emancipated women are depicted as virile and conscientious workers. Associations of women, with well-functioning, modern steel machines, have been emphasized in order to demonstrate their alienation from the aesthetic and their new capacity to achieve control over the tempting pleasures of life (leisure is viewed as a marginal activity and a man or woman who has no job in the public sphere is regarded as a 'parasite'). The visual space of the socialist society is inhabited by the new Amazons – they are labelled 'doers', 'fighters', 'functionaries', 'labourers', 'activists', and so on.

In other words, the android image of femininity articulated through the language of the communist ideology – mechanical, and full of revolutionary pathos – has been refined to counteract the aesthetic language of bourgeois representations of women as figures of fashion, consumerism and 'sex parasitism'. The socialist East, being suspicious of the excessive pleasures and sexual freedom of the 'decadent' West, proclaimed its strict control over women's sexuality and eroticism. Chaste, virtuous women have been presented as the symbols of a new spirit of communist-style puritanism and abandonment of passions and desires. Although socialist gender ideology authorized woman as a symbol of technological progress and the incarnation of revolutionary energy (these goals were manifest particularly in the period of early socialism of the 1950s and the 1960s), women's 'appropriation' of a progressive masculine discourse was not to their benefit but rather functioned to curb a 'transgressive femininity'.

In addition, the discourse of 'sexual equality' and 'equal rights' has been constituted in order to guarantee the system's 'human spirit'. Society framed as a 'system' is also a part of the functional language of socialism. Equality has been manifested through the equal – usually limitless – access to the labour force, to all levels of education and political voting. Furthermore, in the construction of gender identities the inner–outer dichotomy was powerfully mobilized through the nationalist discourse of the totalitarian state.

Turning back to the national history, including the Renaissance and liberation from Ottoman rule, the national question has been always closely connected with the woman question. Whereas in many Western countries during the nineteenth century discussions were concentrated on the political and social participation of women as autonomous and rational individuals, the roles of Bulgarian women were conceptualized around their national engagements. The first women's organizations, founded in the second half of the nineteenth century, 'served the idea of enlightenment and education due to the national consciousness raising'.[8]

In the nationalist rhetoric, 'woman' is an allegory of interiority, innerness, home(ness) and purity. In this sense, Chatterjee pays attention to the distinction between the social space as home and as world: 'The world is a treacherous terrain of the pursuit of material interests, where practical considerations reign supreme. It is also typically the domain of the male. The home in its essence must remain unaffected by the profane activities of the material world – and woman is its representation.'[9] Socialist gender ideology has actively exploited the figure of woman as a representative of the true identity uncontaminated by Western influences: it is not surprising that, especially in the late 1970s and the 1980s, the politics of reproduction and regimes of fertility appeared on the political agenda. Women's reproduction was underlined as the 'natural' function, rather than an activity of women, as their duty rather than as their right. The policy on abortion was extremely restrictive because the main duty of a woman was to give birth to the Nation, to the State. 'I give offspring to the State' was a phrase frequently used by women a decade ago. So, even though socialist propaganda proclaimed new types of women's engagements devoted to 'the building of the new society', the images of femininity remained bound within their traditional obligations concerning reproduction and the preservation of the Nation. The newly-formed communal identities based on a loyalty to Party and State have served as a repository for national values and as a counteraction to the external influences from the West. Women are depicted as bearers of 'nativeness' and as markers of the cultural boundaries of the socialist nation-state. Women are the best representatives of collective life and the collective values of socialism – they are named 'national heroines' as mothers, toilers and social activists.

In a similar spirit J. Kristeva points out that women are the best supporters of the social order in Eastern Europe: 'in the East, ... women promoted to decision-making positions suddenly obtain the economic as well as the narcissistic advantages refused them for thousands of years and become the pillars of the existing governments, guardians of the status quo, the most zealous protectors of the established order'.[10] On the other hand, women's experience is much more diverse, complex and contradictory within the generalization that has been made about women as accomplices of the totalitarian regimes and as subjects privileged by the socialist state. Women were neither excluded nor repressed (the thesis that 'women are victims' is not relevant to woman's situation) but does this open up the discursive space for them? Taking into account the processes through which women's interests are constituted, we can pose the question, 'Are women capable of articulating and representing their own interests?' Or, in other words, 'Does woman's self-assertion coincide with the prevailing goals of the totalitarian system characterized by a neglect of individual rights (for the sake of his or her duties) and intolerance of difference (for the sake of sameness)?' Or, by contrast, are not women depicted as victims of moral redemption, symbols of tensions between the modernist and anti-modernist modes of the nationalist narratives?

'Re-invented' Identities: Europe Already Casts its Shadow

This troubling set of questions continues to be relevant in the 1990s, since Bulgaria's political landscape has radically altered. How is the woman question posed or re-defined now, after the upheavals of 1989, when images of the enemy have faded and 'foreignness' is replaced by 'backwardness'? Where once Western Europe played a retrograde role and blocked the progressive steps of the countries beyond the 'Iron Curtain', now it has become a willing standard to be imitated. The reformist aims of a swift recovery for the post-communist East proclaim 'an eternal game of catch-up' in which 'normalization' becomes the key concept of the post-totalitarian language. Do these appeals to rapid modernization confirm the superiority of Western cultural models and can they be regarded as the betrayal of national values? And can the process of 'becoming modern nations' be equated with following the universal Western blueprint of progress and modernization? It is obvious that modernity, becoming the focus of legitimization of Eastern European democratic projects, cannot be viewed as a concept with 'a single and universally acknowledged meaning'.[11] Apparently, the rhetoric of the 'us–them' divide cannot be ignored in the emergence of the new nation-states in Eastern Europe because of the difference between Eastern and Western nationalisms. As

Chatterjee states, Western nationalisms are rooted in their 'sense of Autochthony' and ability to produce original models, while Eastern nationalisms are always forced to appropriate something foreign to their own cultures in order to become modern.[12]

The situation of women in Bulgaria after 1989 can be defined as being determined by the two main discourses. On the one hand, there is the 'return to the home' discourse. This discourse is not explicitly expressed by the main left- and right-wing political parties, by policy-makers or in the mass media. But it has been facilitated by such factors as demographic depopulation and xenophobic tendencies (a decreasing birth rate for Bulgarians and a continuing high birth rate in the ethnic minority groups), high female rates of unemployment and a restricted labour market for women and the cutting back of widespread child-care centres and increases in fees. The negative effects of the socialist model of women's emancipation resulted in a double burden, low earnings, deterioration of health indicators and so on. Although two-year paid maternity leave, employment protection for mothers and medical benefits for children are still protected by law, in practice a lot of women have lost their maternity benefits owing to the expansive closure and privatization of the state-run enterprises.

On the other hand, the discourse of 'westernization' and 'normalization' of the country has been explicated through messages concerned with implementing 'European' standards and models. The latter should also include governmental 'policy' toward women, and especially vulnerable groups of women such as single and divorced mothers, disabled women, low-skilled and poorly-educated women and women in ethnic minorities. Enormous support for these groups may also come from non-governmental organizations (NGOs), but the process of their establishment has been seriously hindered by re-emerging nationalistic and regional politics. Until now there have been only a few women's NGOs in Bulgaria, which are trying to speak up about special women's programmes and to warn the public of the violation of women's rights on the labour market and in the home, and in the generation of new laws that discrimine against women. However, in general, in the context of weak 'pro-civil society' ideology these NGOs are elitist, their influence in society is very constrained and their mobilization role is slight.

Thus, women's self-conceptualizations have been constructed at the intersection of these two conflictual discourses and social practices. The new conditions created by the transition to a market economy have resulted in deepening impoverishment and deterioration of living standards for a great proportion of women. An 'average' Bulgarian woman has a higher education level than compared with an 'average' man but usually she does a less-qualified job and receives lower payment. The strategy for survival at any price, whatever it might mean – looking for any kind of job, even prostitution, using discarded food and clothes, producing home-made food, relying on the state for benefits and close relatives' support – has mainly been displayed in households headed by women and in marginalized groups of women from the Turkish and Roma (Gypsy) communities.[13] Bearing in mind the recent situation which threatens human survival, how do women in Bulgaria conceptualize themselves? How are new articulations of gender roles, alongside the influential socialist gender ideology, incorporated into and constitutive of the individual statements gained in empirical studies?

Empirical Findings

In the following pages I present the main findings from a survey carried out in 1997.[14] The field research was conducted among a sample of 190 women who were recruited from the three main ethnic communities: ethnic Bulgarians, Turkish and Gypsy women. The latter represent the two largest ethnic minorities in the country. The Bulgarian interviewees were mainly drawn from the population of Sofia while the respondents from the two other groups were from the countryside, where they are mainly located. Additionally, the sample was composed according to economic status, age and educational level. The influence of these factors on the nature of women's identities has been hypothesized.[15]

The socio-demographic profile of each ethnic group studied is quite different but relevant to the specificity of the ethnos, although the official statistical information concerning ethnic minority communities has been incomplete and deficient for the past three decades. The socialist state proclaimed no need to collect such data because of its politics of assimilation of all minorities in the 'united Bulgarian nation'. However, data from the 1992 Census show that most of the Turkish and Roma populations live in rural areas, unlike most of the ethnic Bulgarians who are mainly in urban situations. The age structures of the populations from both minority communities also differ from that of the ethnic Bulgarians. The demographic profiles of the former have been characterized by pre-industrial types of demographic behaviour, that is, high fertility (with four, five and six children) and high mortality rates, while the ethnic Bulgarians maintain low birth rates (one or two children) and high life expectancy (74 years for women, 67 years for men). Owing to their peculiar religious and cultural characteristics, the Turkish and the Roma women tend to marry young – the former after completion of secondary school and the latter at the age of 14–15 and even younger.[16] After the collapse of communism most of the uneducated women lost their low-skilled jobs and became long-term unemployed. They also lost their chance to receive state paid maternity leave and became frequent clients of the social welfare system.

According to the above-mentioned characteristics of the ethnic groups studied, among the Bulgarian respondents the majority are university graduates; in the Turkish sample the dominant proportion consists of women with a secondary school; and the highest share of the Roma respondents have elementary schooling. Relatively, the proportion of non-working women is much higher in both minority groups, especially in the Gypsy one.

The questionnaire includes 73 questions divided into two types: with fixed answers and open-ended.[17] The analysis that follows is based on the questions concerning the research theme of female identity and gender stereotypes. Most of the questions relating to this topic are in open-ended format in order to allow respondents to express their views in their own language. In particular, the interviewers in the local ethnic minorities were instructed to write down the immediate responses to the open-ended questions. Afterwards, two researchers read the interviewees' answers and classified them into different categories. The new categories obtained presented interviewees' choices according to their most frequently used words and phrases. Finally, the categories were recoded and were ready for statistical processing.

In response to the question 'What is the main source of a woman's well-being?'*, 56.8 per cent give the answer 'to prosper in her professional career'. The other alternatives – 'descent from an affluent family', 'a rich and influential husband' and 'contacts with influential people' – are less frequently declared: respectively by 13.7 per cent, 17.9 per cent and 4.7 per cent of the respondents. The stereotype of woman's well-being as based on her professional efforts was shared by the whole group of women interviewed, irrespective of their educational level, marital and economic status or age. The Turkish women who have a lower educational level also adhered to the stereotype of the independent woman and only the Gypsy women challenged this opinion and gave priority to a husband's and parental wealth. These results do not sound striking in the context of large educational contrasts among women from the three ethnic groups. Data from the 1992 Census reveal that 3.0 per cent of Bulgarians, 16.0 per cent of Turks, and 36.7 per cent of Gypsies have only primary education respectively; 54.0 per cent, 24.6 per cent and 7.8 per cent have secondary, and 20.2 per cent, 2.0 per cent and 0.9 per cent have higher.[18]

Most Gypsy children never start school, or they attend it for no more than two or three years. The situation is somewhat worse for Gypsy girls, whose main responsibilities are to look after younger children and to help in domestic production, so they are forced to remain outside the system of public education. While supporting the view that the family is the main source of woman's well-being, Gypsy answers to the question 'For whom is attainment of higher education more important?'* look quite curious. Support of equal educational attainments for the male and female gender is given by 91.6 per cent of all respondents and is shared across the different educational levels, ethnic backgrounds and economic status of the women interviewed.

Another statement which is supported by a high degree of consensus is related to the question, 'What type of man do you need in your life?'*. 'A man who is my equal partner' is the most frequent answer, given by 59.5 per cent. The answer 'a good father' is placed next by 53.2 per cent, and the two other alternatives – 'one who is willing to do everything for me' and 'one who is my guardian' – are identified respectively by 42.6 per cent and 40.5 per cent.[19] Again, the stereotype of equal partnership is supported by the whole sample of respondents except for those from the ethnic minorities. The Turkish women evaluate most highly a man who is a good father: 66.7 per cent gave this response, whereas the Gypsy women placed a man's ability to protect his wife in first place: 59.3 per cent gave this answer. Here again, the cultural backgrounds concerning ideas of equality rather than those for protection have been strongly emphasized. The higher level of education of the Bulgarian women presumes them to be more tolerant of ideas concerning gender inequality, unlike the less-educated women from minority communities who admire their protected status.

'How would you define an emancipated woman?'**. Two-thirds of the respondents (68.4 per cent) answered this open-ended question using positive responses: for 32.1 per cent emancipation supposes personal independence and self-assurance ('a woman who can alone cope with her problems', 'a woman who knows what she wants and how to achieve it', 'a woman not being dependent on a man by her side', 'a woman who believes in her abilities, the ambitious one'); for 19.5 per cent of the respondents emancipation is described in terms of equality with men ('a woman who has reached equal rights with man', 'an equal partner to a man', 'who has equal right at home and in society', 'socially active woman'); 16.8 per cent define emancipation as equivalent to paid work, financial independence and high education ('economically independent woman', 'highly educated, with ambitions and can survive alone', 'working woman', 'financially independent and who can afford everything'). Only 2.6 per cent express a negative attitude towards emancipation, identifying it through such phrases as an emancipated woman is 'a neglected woman in some sense', 'a woman for everything', 'an expensive luxury', 'a woman deprived of male support'.

Respondents' definitions of woman's emancipation were matched by their self-esteem, as indicated by responses to the question, 'Do you think of yourself as an emancipated woman?'*. Fewer than half of the respondents gave a positive answer (43.7 per cent), almost the same percentage (38.4 per cent) found it difficult to identify themselves, and 17.9 per cent said 'no'. The gap observed between the stereotype of woman's emancipation and incomplete personal identification with it could be interpreted as a result of either the influence of other stereotypes or the erosion of this particular one. Half of the younger women had problems with their self-identities as emancipated women in comparison with older women (aged over 50), who possessed higher self-esteem. Perhaps women from the generation over 50 have centred their identities strongly upon the stereotype of the emancipated woman because of the communist ideology and the state-guaranteed benefits for working women, unlike the younger female generations who are under attack because of the economic recession and governmental lack of concern for women's problems.

To the question, 'For whom would you be inclined to sacrifice yourself?'**, 42.6 per cent mentioned only children and 37.9 per cent underlined only family; only 2.1 per cent placed any stress on the job and professional promotion, 6.3 per cent gave priority to the Nation and Motherland, and 4.2 per cent were not inclined to sacrifice themselves at all. The respondents' answers were expressed briefly in one or two words, and the language was totally precise and absolutely uniform. At the same time, this is the question that evoked the most responses compared with the other open-ended questions; this may be an indicator of the high reception of sacrifice as a mode of behaviour in women's everyday lives. The value of parenthood is also highly stressed in answering other questions. When asked, 'Which is the highest goal in a woman's life?'**, one-third (30.5 per cent) of the whole sample declares in favour of the family ('to raise children', 'to have a good family', 'to bring up a child', 'to be a happy family') and one-third (27.4 per cent) specifies 'mixed' values including mainly family and job ('to have a good family and career', 'self-realization as a wife and a mother and professional promotion', 'to reach a balance between profession and family life').

The position of balance between family and job is supported by the Bulgarian and the Turkish women, whereas the Gypsy women generally respect only the family. The strategy of such balancing has also motivated the answers of the Bulgarians to the question 'Does a mother have to sacrifice herself for her family?'* The answer 'without any doubt' is given by 39.5 per cent for the whole sample (respectively by 53.3 per cent of the Turkish, 51.9 per cent of the Gypsy and 33.8 per cent of the Bulgarian respondents). The next alternative, 'yes, but in a balanced way', is pointed to by the majority of respondents (58.9 per cent). Among them the greatest part are Bulgarian women (63.9 per cent), next are Gypsy (48.1 per cent) and lastly Turkish (46.7 per cent) women. The third alternative, 'no, a woman has her own life', is supported by only 1.6 per cent of the whole group asked. Is this a paradox, that women highly approve of the idea of equality at the same time as praising their sacrifice for children? Or perhaps women's acceptance of equality concerns their attitudes and 'lip service', and in their actual behaviour they follow a different strategy. The answers to other questions clarify this point.

In answer to the question, 'What gives you self-respect as a woman?'**, one-third of all women emphasized relationships, using such phrases as 'good family', 'respect from my relatives and friends', 'that I am a mother', 'my children', 'my husband', 'the love of my family'. Career, profession and economic independence formed the inner core of identity for 16.3 per cent of women. Clothes and good looks were mentioned by only 11.1 per cent. A quarter of all respondents, predominantly in the ethnic minorities, confessed their low self-esteem.

Identities are constructed not only through the inclusion of permissive actions but also through exclusion from the outside. In a culture where family responsibilities, primarily motherhood, are evaluated highly, women's behaviour is under strict control. Many researchers point to gender asymmetry in this field, stressing the more restrictive attitudes toward girls and women compared with the looser demands made of boys and men.[20] What women are not allowed – in other words, sanctions and forbidden behaviour – are constitutive of the ingredients of self-identity: for example, 'What would your close relatives not be inclined to forgive you as a woman?'** In answering this question, the greatest part of the respondents (33.7 per cent) pointed to 'an irresponsible attitude toward the family'. 'Adultery' is placed second by 21.1 per cent, although for the Gypsy community it is considered to be the main taboo for women. 'Betrayal, deception, arrogance and selfishness' are put in third place by 14.7 per cent. 'To be independent, to be ambitious, to behave like a man' was underlined by only 5.3 per cent. Obviously, the spectrum of limits for women's behaviour concerns only their manifestation in the family and is directed to the preservation of its boundaries.

With regard to the question, 'What makes you feel most devalued as a woman?'**, the responses given were classified mainly into two groups according to the respondents' ability to identify the source of unfair treatment. The greater part, 37.4 per cent, report abstract positions labelled as 'neglect', 'lack of respect', 'arrogance', 'lack of rights', 'distrust', 'dishonesty', 'disdain', 'insulting behaviour', 'not respecting my opinion', without specifying the agents and sites of under-valuation. The other group of statements, given by 33.7 per cent, are more concrete: 'brutal behaviour of some men', 'being perceived only as sexual object', 'a despotic attitude on the part of the "strong sex"', 'a lack of voice in the family', 'to be treated only as a domestic servant', 'not being respected by husband and children', 'sexual harassment by my boss', 'men's flirtation and mockery', 'when I am told I am too young to start a job'. For 6.3 per cent, women's indignity is rooted in poverty: 'money deficiency', 'misery', 'empty pockets', 'lack of minimum of living conditions', 'the fact that we work a lot but receive nothing as a reward', 'lack of the wherewithal to live a normal social life'. The answers pictured in this way did not vary across education, age or status of the women asked, but they did differ for the women from ethnic minority communities. The Turkish women place the family as the main site of women's indignity, and at the opposite end of this viewpoint, the women from Gypsy communities feel mistreated mainly by society or are embarrassed to articulate the subject in concrete terms.

In answering this question, 'What are you afraid of?'*, most of the respondents point to different frustrations: physical violence – 63.2 per cent; moral abuse – 50.3 per cent; robbery in the street – 55.8 per cent; robbery at home – 63.2 per cent; rape – 58.2 per cent; deception – 47.6 per cent. Women from the ethnic minority communities feel anxious to a greater extent than the Bulgarian women: 59.1 per cent of the Bulgarian respondents, 66.7 per cent of the Turkish women and 81.5 per cent of the Gypsy women fear physical violence; respectively 43.2 per cent, 66.7 per cent, and 66.7 per cent fear moral abuse; 47.7 per cent, 76.7 per cent, and 74.1 per cent cited robbery in the street; 58.3, 76.7 per cent, and 74.1 per cent answered by mentioning robbery at home; 50.8 per cent, 73.3 per cent, and 77.8 per cent fear rape; and 40.9 per cent, 53.3 per cent, and 74.1 per cent mentioned deception.

When considering age, in response to the question, 'When does a woman grow old?'**, in the perceptions of the Bulgarian respondents age is constructed predominantly as a matter of mentality: 42.9 per cent define ageing as 'lack of interest in life'. Such a position is taken by half as many respondents in the Turkish (23.3 per cent) and in the Gypsy (18.5 per cent) samples. In the definitions of women in the ethnic minoritiy, ageing has a physiological meaning and is fixed to a concrete age. For the Turkish respondents, women grow old at the age of 60 while for the Gypsy women this process comes earlier at the age of 45–50. So the sense of ageing is quite specific for each minority ethnic community, being rooted in the anthropology of women's 'roles'. The life cycle for the Roma and the Turkish women is perceived as going into its decline alongside the ending of their productive 'roles', whereas for the ethnic Bulgarian women, ageing is viewed beyond its biological meaning. In addition, perceptions of ageing are very relevant to the different age structures of the varous ethnic populations. While 22.2 per cent of the ethnic Bulgarians are in the age groups of 60 and over, only 11.6 per cent of the Turks and 5.1 per cent of the Gypsies reach this age.[21]

Some Conclusions

In trying to delineate the centre and the peripheries of women's self-identity in the post-communist era in Bulgaria, I started with two premises. First, that socialist gender ideology is still alive, and second, that the new images of women provoked by new realities will be shaped and presented in the public sphere. One of the preliminary hypotheses to be empirically validated concerned some variations in self-conceptualizations of women from different generations, educational levels and ethnic backgrounds. It was assumed that young female generation of 20–30-year-old women would re-evaluate their grandmothers' and mothers' roles, to review the balancing of work and parenting, thereby reinventing their new life strategies.

Although in the first part of this study I considered the political construction of womanhood during the socialist regime, I did not touch upon the issue of what the mechanisms are through which symbolic violence is fabricated. In a contribution of this length I cannot elaborate on this question, but I do wish to point out the conclusion that the discourse of an emancipated woman has been constitutive of the respondents' images of womanhood. As Gramsci says, 'hegemonic' discourse does not impose itself on consciousness in a coercive way; it is always accepted through making it more comfortable and sensible to our everyday life. Women were being flattered by the state with this idea of equality during the past five decades. Whether acknowledged or not by women, the myth of equality allowed them to take pride in their quasi-feminist roles. This probably explains why the preliminary idea about age and educational differentiation was not confirmed. On the contrary, a high degree of convergence of self-identification strategies among Bulgarian women from different generations and educational backgrounds was observed. The only divergent self-identification strategies were manifested by the women from the ethnic minorities, especially the Gypsy women. Because of the cultural segregation of the Roma people from the rest of Bulgarian soicety, they were not 'infected' with the idea of equality. The process of expanding marginalization of this community since the 1990s, implying mass unemployment and alcoholism, a sharp decline in school attendance and increases in criminality and deviant behaviour, is likely to stimulate further disintegration of the Roma population which will have unfavourable effects on the position of Roma women.[22]

The second conclusion based on these empirical findings can be expressed in the following way. Although approving of gender equality and an ideology of emancipation on an abstract level, women predominantly identify themselves with mothering and caring within the family. The respondents' vocabulary is much more accurate and elaborate when women define themselves in relation to others in their responses to the questions concerning the prohibited zones of behaviour, sacrifices, and the highest goals in a woman's life. The questions that reveal women's self-esteem, sense of dignity, individual emancipation or unfair treatment are 'silenced' by almost one-third of the respondents. This lack of articulation could imply that women do obscure their 'personal' needs for the sake of the recognition received from the others. Thus, respondents' predominant affiliations with the family make it possible to conceive of female subjectivity 'in spatial terms',[23] where the family has mapped the borders of 'spatial existence'.

Family responsibilities as constitutive of the core of today's women's self-identities have been motivated not only through the ideology of returning mothers to their homes. Incidentally, the socialist regime never advocated such a position, paradoxically imposing on women an ambivalent standard: to be good mothers and to be good workers. That is why a strategy of balancing their time between family and activities outside the family was outlined by the respondents as the most preferable. On the other hand, in trying to understand women's paramount identification with the family it is not possible to escape the theme of sacrifice. The mother–saint–martyr model has been widely presented in Bulgarian fiction and ethnographic writings.[24] The myth of women's sacrifice, presented by the folk image of the 'built-in bride', could be used as an interpretative key to imagine even present-day visions and identifications of Bulgarian women. In the situation of a radical reorganization of public institutions and blocking of women's access to influential public positions, the family becomes the only alternative arena in which to invest personal energy. Thus, sacrifice understood in terms broader than its literal meaning is assumed to be the only legitimate female culture (power of the powerless) in conditions where personal freedom and choice are restricted.

These empirical results have corresponded to similar findings from other national surveys in the 1990s which have drawn the conclusions that, on the one hand, women in Bulgaria are highly motivated to engage in paid work and to balance work and family at the price of their personal interests and even health; on the other hand, personal qualities as independence, autonomy, ambitions are less valued by the women in comparison with security and guarantees from the state. Using these empirical results and my personal observations, I think a conclusion can be drawn that women in Bulgaria at the close of the twentieth century are trapped in their past through the myths of equality and emancipation and in their present through the poverty, passivity and lack of awareness of their own specific interests.

Obviously, these pitfalls challenge the idea that the new post-communist realities in Bulgaria might have forced reconceptualizations of women's identities. Whether changing or remaining the same, ordinary women's voices should be taken into account by women's NGOs, experts, policy-makers and all those agents who want to improve women's status in the newly-emerging societies in Central and East European countries.

NOTES

1. T. De Lauretis, (1987) *Technologies of Gender* (Bloomington, IN: Indiana University Press, 1987), p.136.
2. H. Bhabha, *The Location of Culture* (London: Routledge, 1994), p.162.
3. S. Suleri, 1991. 'Woman Skin Deep: Feminism and the Postcolonial Condition', *Critical Inquiry*, Vol.18, No.1 (1991), p.761.
4. G. Bhattacharyya, 'Who Fancies Pakis?' in S. Ledger, J. McDonagh and J. Spencer (eds.), *Political Gender (Texts and Contexts)* (Hemel Hemstead: Harvester–Wheatsheaf, 1994), p.86.
5. G. Spivak, *The Post-Colonial Critic* (London: Routledge, 1991).
6. S. Hall, 'Who Needs "Identity"?', in S. Hall and P. du Gay (eds.), *Questions of Cultural Identity* (London: Sage, 1997), p.4.
7. Hall, 'Who Needs "Identity"?'
8. J. Deimel, 'Bewegte Zeiten. Frauen in Bulgarien Gestern und Heute', dissertation (Munich: LDV-Verlag, 1998).
9. P. Chatterjee, 'The Nationalist Resolution of the Women's Question', in Kum-Kum Sungari and Sudesh Vaid (eds.), *Recasting Women: Essays in Colonial History* (New Delhi: Kali for Women, 1989), p.238.
10. J. Kristeva, 'Women's Time', in T. Moi (ed.), *The Kristeva Reader* (Oxford: Basil Blackwell, 1986), p.201.
11. R. Felski, 'The Gender of Modernity', in Ledger, McDonagh and Spencer (eds.), *Political Gender*, p.152.
12. Chatterjee, as quoted in R. Radhakrishnan, 'Nationalism, Gender, and the Narrative of Identity', in A. Parker, M. Russo, D. Sommer and P. Yaeger (eds.), *Nationalisms and Sexualities* (London: Routledge, 1992), p.86.
13. International Labour Organization, *Women in Poverty: Evaluation of Politics and Strategies for Decrease of Poverty in Bulgaria* (Geneva: ILO Bulgaria: UNDP, 1998).
14. The survey was part of the project 'Marginality and Integrity: Constructing Gender Identities in Post-Communist Bulgaria', financed by the Research Support Scheme, Open Society Institute (grant No. 716/1996).
15. According to economic status, four groups have been distinguished: (1) working women; (2) non-working women who do not work either because of loss of their job or because they are on maternity leave; (3) young female students; (4) retired women. Three age groups are isolated: (1) 18–19; (2) 30–49; (3) 50 and over. By educational levels the sample was divided into three categories: (1) incomplete elementary and elementary; (2) incomplete secondary and secondary; (3) incomplete higher and complete higher. Although the sample is not representative, all these factors can be controlled by statistical manipulation.
16. I. Tomova, *The Gypsies in the Transition Period* (Sofia: International Center for Minority Studies and Intercultural Relations, 1995).
17. In the text below, the questions with fixed responses are marked by '*', and open-ended questions by '**'.
18. National Statistical Institute Data, 1992.
19. The total sum of all answers exceeds 100 per cent because of the multiple choice of answering.

20 B. Reeves-Ellington, 'A Woman's Place in Bulgaria: Past Perspectives, Current Realities', paper presented to the National Women's Studies Association Conference, Skidmore College, New York , 12–16 June 1996.
21. National Statistical Institute Data, 1992.
22. Tomova, *The Gypsies in the Transition Period.*
23. L. Grossberg, (1997) 'Identity and Cultural Studies – Is That All There Is?' in Hall and du Gay (eds.), *Questions of Cultural Identity*, p.101.
24. I. Khadzhiyski, *Bit i dushevnost na nashiya narod* [Lifestyle and Mentality of Our People] (Sofia: Bulgarski pisatel, 1974).

New Dimensions of the Sexual Universe: Sexual Discourses in Russian Youth Magazines

ELENA OMEL'CHENKO

Study of three new Russian youth journals clearly charts shifts in the understanding of gender differences in Russian youth culture at the end of the 1990s. There exists a clear trend regarding the exploitation of the idea of a 'new gender revolution', including the fragmentation of the search for sexual identity, specific issues surround individual sexual preference encountered in the post-Soviet moral climate, and the dominant role of the media in the formation of sexual discourses. It is clear that sexuality is a key lever of power in contemporary Russian society and as such a key site of struggle for the youth audience. In this sense Russian youth magazines work at a similar level to those in the West. In contrast to the West, however, non-traditional sexualities are employed in Russian youth magazines as a challenge to the youth audience and in a way which links sexuality to wider philosophical and ideological quests.

This consideration of the formation and representation of sexuality and gender stereotypes arises from a study conducted over the past three years of texts devoted to contemporary youth cultures and subcultures.[1] The aim is to compare Western (mostly British) and Russian academic research and interpret changes that have taken place in youth cultures at the end of the 1990s. Studying youth cultures as represented in publications for Russian youth suggests that, despite differences in genre and quality, there is a clear trend towards the exploitation of the idea of a 'new gender revolution'. Although in itself nothing new, it is certainly novel in the context of Russian life and is manifested in these magazine articles in discussions of what it is to be contemporary men and women; ways and forms of social and cultural interpretation of reality (masculine, feminine or mixed); symbols and signs that define one's attitude to gender and its socially acceptable demonstrations; Western and Russian modes of behaviour; and 'traditional' patriarchal as well as shockingly innovative ideas about gender.

While accepting that there may well be a gap between journalists' understandings of such questions and the reality of youth practice, this study explores the social and cultural context of these new concepts of gender.

The new Russian youth magazine market is constantly developing. The first stage of the post-*perestroika* press boom was characterized by the appearance on the youth market of a huge number of tabloids, semi-pornographic and pornographic publications that were openly meant to scandalize their audience and had a marginal cultural status. The second stage was linked to the publication of Russian versions of international magazines such as *Playboy, Cosmopolitan, Penthouse* and so on. Apart from translations directly made from Western sources, these magazines published Western articles specially edited for Russian youth, as well as their own material. Editorial boards were actively engaged in the search for their own niche among youth audiences in contemporary Russia. The majority of magazines which appeared at this stage were aimed at 'new' Russians and their wives who could only be considered to be 'youth' in formal (age) terms. The third, current, stage is characterized by a gradual disappearance of the openly pornographic publications from the market; the appearance of specialized magazines for the young 'mega-rich'; an increase in popularity of underground and subcultural publications aimed at a very specific audience; and the growth of 'fanzines'.Three youth magazines are analysed in this study: *Om, Ptyuch* and *Rovesnik*.

Om (founded in November 1995; editor-in-chief – Igor Grigoryev) is positioned as a publication for young men and is characterized as a 'serious glossy' magazine. As its editor says, 'Every issue is a snapshot of the 1990s, a collage of the little pieces of today.' It focuses on the upper crust of society describing its social events, private conversations and exclusive entertainments. Sexually it is masculine, obsessed with sex and open about shocking inclinations.

Ptyuch (founded in the spring of 1995; editor-in-chief – Igor Shulinskii) is positioned as a publication for youth (up to 22–25 years old) devoted to youth music culture, mostly to the rave culture of the night clubs. The editors of the magazine present it as an elite publication with its roots in a bohemian past characterized by underground, independence and entertainment. *Ptyuch* aims to stay 'underground' and thus rejects any conscious attempt to appeal to the masses. Its titles are full of shocking expressions: 'cult', 'stylish', 'alternative', 'extreme and ecstasy', 'provocative' and 'offensive', sex, drugs and parties. High fashion, marginal attractions, are also there: graffiti, surfing and skateboards, scandalous films, various sexual practices with a hint of sado-masochism, pornography and buggery.

Rovesnik (established in July 1992; editor-in-chief – Igor Chernyshkov) is an international illustrated monthly magazine for youth aged between 16 and 19, which presents the news about world youth culture (mainly about rock music). *Rovesnik*, the oldest Russian youth magazine, has new supplements: '16', or 'everything you wanted to know about sex but were afraid to ask'; and 'Shtuchka' – a magazine for young women, and 'all the stars', a collection of posters and placards with portraits of the stars of world cinema and pop music. The magazine is 'harmless', with hit parades, rock encyclopedias, fan clubs, musical quiz shows, and happy endings. There are articles on serious subjects: how to continue your education, how to marry happily and how to practise safe sex. If the chosen magazines are classified chronologically they belong to the end of the second and to the beginning of the third stage of the development of the market for youth magazines. For the purposes of analysis I have chosen magazines from the end of 1996 up to mid-1997. The similarity in the sexual discourses of *Om* and *Ptyuch* allows them to be analysed in comparison with each other, whereas *Rovesnik* is analysed separately.

The textual analysis presented here is only the first stage of research, aiming to describe the main parameters of the changing sexual and gender universe of Russian youth cultures at the end of the 1990s as seen through the texts of these three youth magazines. The second stage of research will explore the extent to which these sexual discourses have resonance among youth of various social and cultural strata in provincial Russia and involves the analysis of focus groups, in-depth interviews, and a small-scale express survey of the youth.

The Warriors of the Sexual Front

Within Russian politics obedience to the will of the Soviet state was significant in all spheres of public and private life.[2] The domination of the state extended from the Kremlin to each bedroom. The sexual sphere was the last resort of one's individual choice, and in that respect it was in the zone of most serious attention from the new moralists and ideologists. In that respect the 'liberation' of women under the Soviet regime could be seen as a specifically Soviet transformation of gender relations, the aim of which was to subdue men and women. Women received a 'gift from the state', the freedom to work on a par with men. Men were given a role of the 'second husband', after the state. One of the consequences of this alliance of women with the Soviet state against men was that a very serious 'husband-censor' of private (including sexual) relations appeared. At the ideological level women demonstrated their attractiveness to the state. They wanted to please the state, to be beautiful for the state, to be faithful to the state and to bring up children for the state.

The demise of the Soviet regime symbolically signified the divorce between the state and its women. The state stopped loving its wives, women, children and young people as it had done before. It rejected the idea of maintaining order in families, the idea of bringing up the future generations properly. However, at the practical level both men and women still enjoy waiting for 'special privileges' because the system of the old gender stereotypes turned out to be resilient. The patriarchal layer of gender culture still remains and one can find it in a special form even in the most modern search for new dimensions of sexual and gender discourse.

The process of changes, shifts or replacements of gender stereotypes is best observed in the mass media. Texts directed at youth audiences demonstrate what happens when the state ceases to dictate gender ideology and allows it to remain outside censorship and to become a 'game'. Analysis of the mass media is also interesting because gender discourse is formed here more freely (because it is still a game), outside the realities of family life and the problems of reproduction. Unlike the live phenomena of Russian youth cultures, these texts demonstrate a different type of gender and sexual practice. These texts do not seek to interact with real people's lives. Instead they appear to play with gender, they test it, they check it and try on various sexual and gender 'clothes'.

If we examine this 'battlefield' in detail we shall see a certain resemblance of carnival. At this carnival we meet not only elements of the Soviet system, plus elements of the market economy, but also Western and Russian youth cultures. It is not only a replacement of the old set of values with new ones but also a mixture of Russian models with Western models. It is in media discourses that we most clearly see the formation of contemporary youth gender identity. The analysis of journalists' texts helps us to observe the nature and methods of transformation of the main ideas of the Western gender discourse into the Russian mass media. It seems that the disappearance of gender constructions is happening right before our eyes, which confirms once again that gender is not a state but a process.

Youth and Sexuality: The End of the Millennium and Looking to the Future

The end of the twentieth century and of the second millennium could be rightly called the celebration of youth cultures. Practically all youth sub-cultures of the twentieth century are experiencing some form of renaissance. Many authors who try to discern some contours of the future draw their energy from the idea of youth. Nobody knows for certain whose values and disposition will serve as a foundation for the new world in the twenty-first century, and whether the next generation will remotely resemble the youth of today. Some searches for signs of the future lead us to 'trendy ideologists' – the cult people of today's youth. It is possible that it is their practices, which look new today, that will become the order of tomorrow. Contemporary youth cultures mostly revolve around the desire to theatricalize the melancholy and boring 'everyday' existence. The end of the century appears as a perfectly suitable time for this search:

> This spring in Paris the clock has been started which counts the last 1,000 days up to the year 2000. They say that the last millennium will start 350 days later, but the discreet charm of round figures and the child-like joy because of the fact that the number becomes smaller every day makes people feel the so-called pre-millennium tension. (*Om*, Dec. 1996)

Micro-Revolutions to Replace the Stormy Ones

In the magazines analysed, many texts are devoted to the new ideas of the 1990s. According to the authors of these texts, their ideas will form the shape of the future. *Om* magazine calls these ideas 'revolutionary' because they have changed the cultural space at the end of the century. *Ptyuch* magazine calls them the maladies of the world, but in their foundations these ideas are quite similar. Publishing their cultural and ideological manifestos almost simultaneously, in May and June 1997, these magazines were waging a hidden argument with each other. Table 1 lists ideas devoted to new fantasies on the subject of youth sexuality in these two magazines.[3]

The End of the Century and the New Sensuality

What is new as a foundation for a new way of life and a new quality of sexuality? The end of the century and of the millennium is not merely a time barrier. Since it is impossible to foresee the exact shape of the future, the desire to be super-sceptical and cynical towards contemporary values has been born, along with the desire to create something absolutely new. Therefore it is viewed as extremely important to forget about the old illusions, about the possibility of any moral definitions. The twentieth century had too many moral searches, hence a 'clean' foundation is needed for the beginning of a new century.

A Healthy and Consistent Cynicism

In *Om* the end of the century is treated as precursor of cynicism. This means the denial of everything definite, which demands not only the liberation from sex but also the mockery of this liberation. The departure from fanatical service to ideas, the struggle for the purity of genre, allows us to get rid of cheap fakes and take cynicism to its logical conclusion.Ugliness and suffering are on a par with beauty, such that the banal concept of

TABLE 1

REVOLUTIONARY IDEAS AT THE END OF THE 1990s

	Om	Ptyuch
Name	Revolutionary ideas of the 1990s	Maladies of the world in the 1990s
Source	1. The proximity of genders as a new strategy for recreation and a favourite idea of stylists 2. A new concept of masculinity. The image of white heterosexuals who suffer because they don't want to become grown-up men. 3. Homosexuality. The politically correct homosexuals have turned from being radicals to becoming part of a shopping list, from a dark sub-culture they moved into a shining niche in the market.	1. Unisex – The desire to get rid of your own sex. Your role model is the adolescent of the opposite sex.
Leisure and pleasure as a lifestyle	5. Adrenaline – part of life. Search for natural varieties of spiritual pleasures, up to facing the death. Longing for risk. 6. Infantilism. The adults started to collect toys. The process of becoming a grown-up has turned into a children's game.	2. Hedonism – Every minute of life should bring you pleasure. The hedonist of the 90s knows the styles of contemporary music in detail. He knows about drugs and how to plan his or her time. 3. Infantilism. The grown-ups sport openly childish and bright clothes. Ravers like ugly, cuddly toys.
Elements of new ideology	7. Post-political correctness. The struggle of sexes has turned into a bun-fight. 8. A fit of rage. Violence on the roads, in the cinema, impatience, frustration and unprovoked rage, the increase in unmotivated violence. Unpredictable and fatal cruelty has created a new culture of the victim. 9. The artificial naturalness. The transition to naturalness has been reflected in straight hair, pale lips and transparent androgyny.	4. Techno-spiritualism – New technologies, new-age philosophies, psychedelic drugs will save mankind. 5. Decadence. The maniacal division of life into decades, with maniacal generalizations. The tendency is not new but it has reached its peak in the 90s. Maybe because the next decade will be called '00'. 6. The artificial genuineness. One has to look natural in all circumstances.

Note: In the list of *Om* magazine, four ideas out of 11 are directly linked to the changes in gender, to the mixture of sexual roles and qualities. In the list of *Ptyuch* magazine five ideas out of ten depend on new technocratic tendencies and the Internet. *Om* is creating a new concept of homosexuality, whereas *Ptyuch* works on a new theory of techno-hedonism. These manifestos reflect the victorious progression of the gender revolution, which has led to significant shifts in traditional concepts of sex and sexual practices and has turned the subject of homosexuality into a popular product. Both magazines, openly or discreetly, exploit the subject of mixed gender which attracts the attention of curious readers.

harmony and quiet pleasure is made redundant. This will become the source of a new sexuality. In its foundations one can find a destruction of moral taboos related to virtue, truth, beauty, harmony – everything that is given to one by the right of birth, one's body, sex, nation or age. This destruction is closely linked to a new birth of love which has no size, length, age or sex limits and which makes national peculiarities doubtful (*Om*, July–Aug. 1997).

The fashion for healthy cynicism is used by bohemian youth in an attempt to defend their position against the waves of 'pop-ism' of the mass of youth. This trend has been formed in response to a charge of anti-energy which has been accumulating during the past century (in various youth cultures it has developed in different ways). This anti-energy consists of protests and disappointments, hopes and complete despair. Every sub-culture, after it had finished with its underground period, leaves to its successors a 'terrifying' heritage of 'antis': the colour black, fascist symbols, androgyny, chauvinism, new obscenities, famous rock hits, conquered parts of social space, publications for the youth, discotheques, clubs, cafes, pubs and so on. The transformation of youth subcultures into the mainstream, the transformation of its ideas and values into something popular, which is accepted by everybody, has always spread among its true supporters an incredible anger towards the mass media and fashion industries which circulated their practices on a nation-wide scale and made well-marketable pop symbols out of them: 'The cynicism of our generation is not necessarily expressed in shocking words such as Fuck You All. It is expressed mostly through the way of life which cultivates impulsive acts ... I like it, hence I'm behaving correctly' (*Om*, April 1997).

This cynicism turns the transformation of all customary values into a complete and holistic outlook. If subcultures in the 1960s and 1970s merely flirted with gender, if their main forces were directed at this sexual liberation ('natural' revolution), the youth at the end of 1990s, according to an interpretation of their ideologists, cannot be satisfied with this. They demand not only liberation from natural and social limits of the present – they demand the mockery of this liberation:

> Fear becomes attractive; the original notion of sin and virtue has become obsolete mostly because of the fashion for healthy cynicism, the quality without which any young person could be called vulgar. Instead of angelic noses and mouths of children one can imagine phalluses, anuses and vaginas ... Instead of healthy sports – battered and bruised faces with blood on them. Instead of secrets of happy family life – mysteries of untraditional sex. (*Om*, May 1997)

This healthy cynicism, according to the contributors to *Om*, is characterized by an imperceptible border between open rudeness and filth and the humour which they evoke. Cynicism is a public demonstration of soullessness as a counterbalance to 'boring' romanticism. There are no subjects that are forbidden; any ban could be imposed only on their discursive mode. As surrogates of these new trends have appeared, a struggle for the purity of the genre is demanded: the true, 'pure' cynics therefore need to be able to decode the 'cryptographic writing':

> A trendy term has appeared – ambivalence (a latent bi-sexuality or factual lack of specific sexual attraction). It only adds charm in high society. The most youthful magazine *Ptyuch* has been forming ideas about 'amorfus androginus' all the way. Now the subject is thoroughly examined by women's magazines such as *Cosmo*. The main principle of contemporary young men is complete unscrupulousness. Cynicism is a special cryptographic writing which helps this generation to talk. (*Om*, April 1997)

Om points to British culture as a main source and part of cynicism, referring in particular to the artistic practice of the Chapman brothers.[4] One can find in their pictures 'Little children with tender faces with penises instead of noses, with anuses and vaginas instead of mouths ... There hasn't been a work of art before which would exploit scopophilia (getting sexual pleasures through observation and the process of watching) in this way' (*Om*, May 1997). One's ability to enjoy ugliness and suffering serves as a new original source of sexual excitement. In its foundations one can find sadistic and masochistic complexes. For example, St. Sebastian might become an example of eroticism in which one's eyes become the most erogenous zone and the mechanism of observation explains how desire, excitement and pleasure follow one's repulsion. As a domestic variety of cynicism, *Om* presents 'kakbyism' (pretence) and 'pofigism' (indifference):

> During the past six years Russia has been swallowing without chewing everything which the West had been chewing for decades and then, I beg your pardon, belched. The *nouveaux riches* are only apparently [*kak by*] rich. The contemporaneity of a young woman consists in wearing a silly little rucksack. As if she is a globetrotter, a nomad in the 21st Century. Western superficiality, 'kakbyism', acquires the status of the obligatory. (*Om*, Dec. 1996)

If *Om* professes a consistent and healthy cynicism, *Ptyuch* stands for an innocent and exciting form of it. The excitement of the contributors to *Ptyuch* is caused by the fact that its negative charge comes from their mockery of 'American values'.

A Joyful Provocation

Both cynicism and provocation are means of shocking the audience, attempts to be oneself and to do as one pleases. In contrast to cynicism, provocation cannot become fashionable. If rude cynicism ceases to shock, a demonstration of good bourgeois values will become a provocation. The main thing is that one should not be bored: one should have enough courage to be oneself and to do as one pleases in spite of fashion and circumstances: 'Our society has become accustomed to untraditional sex, drugs, green hair. These things are not provocative any more ... If someone could still be shocked by them he or she is a lucky person. A joyful provocation is a driving force of civilization' (*Ptyuch*, 1997, No.3).

A Mixture of Nations, Ages and Sexes as Foundation of a New Social Identification

All nations have become mixed at the end of this century, thanks, in part, to youth cultures which have crossed all borders and barriers and have mixed all tribes and nations of the rebelling youth. Youth cultural practices exist in a global world; they appear as a united multi-coloured interaction. In our epoch when national peculiarities become less and less distinguishable, when one can eat the same food in McDonalds, watch the same film ('Trainspotting', for example) or buy the same clothes (Gap) in London, Moscow and Tokyo, the only way to express individuality is through a concrete personality with its unparalleled store of impressions and physical experiences.

One of the foundations of this cultural globalization, according to the opinion of the contributors to *Om*, is a post-modernist sex industry:

> A sex shop as a source for inspiration is no less significant for the Russian capital than for a foggy London. Let us set aside perverse children, cut-off heads which serve as a material for video cuts and stabbings, sex with animals, quasi-religious performances, cathartic exhibitionism. In that sense Moscow 'wears' the same clothes as London and Tokyo. (*Om*, April 1997)

The leading trend in journalism which comes closest to the chosen subject is a mixture of the sexes and a search for a new concept of homosexuality. This real sexual trend triggers various discussions around such notions as unisex, androgyny and homosexuality in the texts of the magazines. Unisex is a type of demonstration of the sexuality according to which one's sex is not defined. The traditional and customary social concepts of sex are mixed up; boys and girls, men and women dress, smell, look and behave in the same way. This lifestyle is not necessarily supported by unconventional sexual orientations. It is just that femininity and masculinity (whether attached to their masculine or feminine source or not) manifest themselves through the same social symbols and signs. Androgyny is a type of sexuality in which the masculine and the feminine interact in significant measure and coexist in a unique and idiosyncratic combination. Very often these combinations of the traditionally incompatible are demonstrated openly and become the most significant, central component of the style. Homosexuality is a sexual attraction to a member of the same sex.

Unisex: Lived, Lives, Will Live?

A trendy tendency in world culture, called unisex, appeared at the beginning of the 1990s and immediately recruited legions of followers. It has made a great impact on youth and has understandably provoked discussion. The discussions in *Om* are mostly devoted to attempts at predicting the future of this trend. If unisex is only a fashion then its days are numbered. If this is a global transformation of people's concepts about the nature of human sexuality it may become a leading trend in the future. The proximity of the sexes has reached a critical point, and if it goes on like this, sooner or later men and women will exchange places. Let us refer to extracts from the discussion between two very famous and authoritative Russian artists: A. Bartenev (painter) and Yu. Grymov (video-maker and producer) who demonstrate two directly opposite points of view on this subject.

> *Grymov:* Unisex means lack of any love, normal as well as homosexual. It is a half-hearted and utopian idea. When all this was put on an industrial basis, a threat appeared of replacing masculine and feminine sexes by something in between. Unisex is a style and a way of life which is actively and regularly propagated by many famous designers who want to convince their new recruits about the unquestionable superiority of the race of asexual beings. Unisex invariably leads to the end of a human being. Feminism is less dangerous than unisex. I would like to register an anti-unisex party.

> *Bartenev:* Unisex was there already under the Soviets, but this idea wasn't successful.[5] Therefore it wouldn't be possible to unify clothes on a world-wide scale. The fashion for unisex is an oblique legalization of homosexuality, which would have been otherwise impossible to achieve in such a hypocritical society as Russia. In the rest of the world homosexuality enriched culture and science ... love between a man and a woman has emotionally dried up, it doesn't have any novelty and has become a symbol of conservatism. There is a natural gift, a drug – the love which you want ... how can a tie be

masculine or feminine? What gender is a crew cut or a singlet? Getting rid of sexual certainty in clothes, of the silly letters F and M, undoubtedly leads to sexual freedom ... In the very near future the pressure on the unisex will be from the feminine side. Even today women have taken the square toes of the shoes from men, and unisex perfume mostly reminds of female perfume. Women say that they are superior ... More and more often we can see women who wear masculine clothes, don't use any make-up, cut their hair short, behave as men and make as much money as men. All this testifies to the future mixture of sexes, to the change in their places ... And in our country it will happen earlier. There will be huge positive changes in the psychology of the society, because the inner freedom stems from the outer freedom, aesthetic as well as sexual. (*Om*, April 1997)

Ptyuch demonstrates a more optimistic and less ideologically charged view of the fashion for unisex. Provocatively superficial attitudes to the discussion of the burning issues are manifest in the fact that any open and vigorous discussion of the future of unisex is missing from the *Ptyuch* texts: 'The youth of the civilized world have become unisex without exception. It is time for Russia to cross the boundaries, too' (*Ptyuch*, 1997, No.4). The contributors to *Ptyuch* see the deep desire on the part of progressive Russian youth to unify all sides of life as a reason for the wide popularity of this trend. This can help to get rid of clichés of those who control the society and develop new forms of youth solidarity: 'It is obvious that the fashion for uniform satisfies our aesthetic needs in the first place, whereas comfort and practicality have always been only a suitable pretext' (*Ptyuch*, 1997, No.4).

Towards a Homosexual Ideology in Russia

The subject of homosexuality openly or discreetly exists in all issues of the magazines under examination. The only exception is the magazine *Rovesnik* which will be analysed separately. Articles in the magazines are devoted to the search for sources and the social context of homosexual ideology, and to the interpretation of models and devices of homosexual themes as demonstrated in the media.

The most remarkable point in the contemporary domestic motifs about homosexuals as represented by the media is that they have an openly superficial and market-driven character. The concept of 'normal' sexual pleasure is still closely linked to the only possible form, that is sex in the family. It need not necessarily be accompanied by signs of homophobia, such as sharp and irreconcilable denunciations of sexual relationships between persons of the same sex or the struggle with this 'disease'. The problem lies not in the intolerance of the Russian population but in the fact that alternative sexual practices have been less overt and demonstrative than elsewhere. It may also be explained by the Orthodox Christian tradition. Apart from the denunciation of various forms of homosexuality, the desire to experience deeply intimate and hidden feelings of various kinds which should not be made public remains stable. The older the man, the more often he would hear that it is time for him to get married. These words do not express disapproval; rather they demonstrate a sincere compassion, because traditionally it is accepted that only in one's family can one preserve and save oneself. Apart from this, many Russian pop stars on their way to public success attempt directly to copy Western models of theatrical demonstration of homosexuality and use gay aesthetics, up to sado-masochism, in their bid to be at the top of the genre.[6]

Progressive gay aesthetics at the beginning of the 1990s have become a popular Russian cultural mainstream and are not associated in any way whatsoever with sexual deviation. It is not by chance that those magazines that try to uphold their anti-pop image counterpose the search for post-gay concepts to this 'acting as homosexuals'. According to the ideologists for 'pure homosexualism', only the latter can return the question of 'sexual deviancy' back to the underground of contemporary youth culture.

Homosexuals, the 'New Gay' Concept and Russian Cinema

The often-used definition of 'homosexual' is not always precise because it could equally incorporate gays and lesbians – men and women who are attracted by members of the same sex. However in *Om* magazine only masculine homosexuality is analysed, because this magazine is mostly orientated to a masculine audience.

This type of sexuality is examined on the basis of homosexual motives in world and Russian cinema. One of the main problems of the analysis of homosexuality in cinema is that it is very often hidden, because of the nature of this art. *Om* gives several graphic examples of their interpretations of relevant cinematic images:

> A respectable encyclopaedia of the cinema by Efraim Katz (a second edition of it was published in 1994) has a lengthy article on gay and lesbian cinema and talks about the possibility of the creation of films about homo-erotically orientated people by those directors who are not homo-erotic themselves, but it does not explain the subtle situation when non-heterosexual motives are given by way of hint, hypothetically, with presumption. (*Om*, Oct.–Nov. 1996)

In the eyes of Russian artists, homosexuality is not something super-exotic and alien; it is widely known that Sergei Paradzhano, a legendary Soviet film director, was gaoled for being a homosexual:

> It is more complicated with Sergei Eisenstein who is considered as gay in the West but in the USSR this was confined to the rumours about the attraction of the great reformer of the cinema to boys and his death in his bathroom after having sex with one of them. There is a subtle play with unorthodox sexual techniques in 'Ivan the Terrible'. Similarly, A. Tarkovskii subtly treated the complicated and strange relationship between Andrei Rublev and Daniil Chernyi. (*Om*, Oct.–Nov. 1996)

According to the contributors to *Om*, world cinema as a whole could be called a manual for homosexual beginners, because the number of films with homo-erotic motives has been doubling each decade after the 1970s.

In these magazines one can find a real 'hymn to buggery'. This will attract the readers who wish to know more about the pre-history of homosexuality. Although this article talks about Ancient Greece, one can feel that there is a tendency in the narration to modernize the message:

> Today an attractive and sophisticated adolescent could be called a poof, virtually by anyone. However, not so recently homosexuality used to be a synonym of masculinity. People used to think that wisdom could be transmitted from the older man to the younger with the help of a masculine liquid. Blow-jobs used to be the most widespread recipe: instead of a motherly breast, a boy would take the penis of his teacher in his mouth and would have to bring him pleasure. This custom was popular in many tribes during the Stone Age, but it received intellectual support in Greece. Homosexual contacts as a way of upbringing were considered so highly sophisticated that they were regarded as appropriate to aristocrats only. Slaves were denied this pastime. (*Om*, Oct.–Nov. 1996)

The approach of *Ptyuch* magazine to the subject of homosexuality has something in common with that of *Om*. However, it has its own specific elements, too. The common aspect is the assessment of specific transmutations of gay concepts and gay practices in the 1990s: the commercialization of the image of the mysterious and sinful homosexual or transvestite, the gradual transformation of the underground style into pop culture, the unassuming and superficial exploitation of tragic life stories of homosexuals. A consequence of it all is the spread of homophobia: 'The subject of homosexuality has developed in America from complete denial to complete acceptance, lost its value and as a cheap prostitute has given itself away to middle-class taste' (*Ptyuch*, 1997, No.1).

A necessary condition of the normal attitude to the subject of homosexuality is a struggle with the narrow approach to homosexuals as ill and wretched people, which is often demonstrated by the heterosexual majority:

> People's attitude to the subject of homosexuality has always been marked by an insulting sympathy to gay people. The struggle against such sympathy within heterosexual society has united several gifted directors who broke the narrow limits of special gay festivals and have advanced to the forefront of cult world cinema with a slogan 'new queer cinema'. However, if the lack of acceptance of the public could have become a pitfall for them earlier, these days, on the contrary, they could be blamed in being driven by the market. In the years following the Stonewall, homosexuality has become one of the most marketable subjects. (*Ptyuch*, 1997, No.5)

New American cinema is presented as the end of politically correct cinema in which it was enough to be gay, Black, feminist or Latin American in order to deserve serious consideration. This is not enough now because 'true art' speaks to everybody and to prove one's artistic validity any additional market-driven arguments are not necessary: 'The world is not divided into White and Black men and women, the homos and the heteros any more' (*Ptyuch*, 1996, No.9).

In contrast to *Om*, in *Ptyuch* a great deal of space is devoted to letters from readers. The selection of readers' letters to their favourite magazine for publication is never made by chance, therefore the texts of these letters could be rightly seen as part of the discourse of the magazine. The homosexual theme is represented here widely and idiosyncratically. It is marked by exciting tones strongly spiced by obscenities and detailed descriptions of stories about seduction and quest for true – meaning homosexual – love: 'I am grateful to God that he made me a queer. I'm so happy!' (*Ptyuch*, 1997, No.1).

The description of one's feelings is strongly reminiscent of public masturbation: it's a very touching, exciting attitude to oneself, full of love as well as concentration on all nuances of one's sexual experience and pleasure. This is how a 100 per cent heterosexual man confesses his experience as a 'poof':

> Every man wants to be screwed and feel as a women at least once in his life. All my concepts about my own sexuality have changed and now I know that the expression 'to do everything through one's arse' [a Russian idiomatic expression which means 'to do everything carelessly'] is not altogether negative. Still, I needed quite some time

to make my way from 'penis' to 'anus' and take a different attitude to my behind which, as it turned out, can give lots of pleasures. (*Ptyuch*, 1996, No.9)

In contrast to *Om*, *Ptyuch* pays attention to lesbians. Several reports are devoted to journalists' visits to special clubs in the capital where lesbians gather, to interviews with the 'leaders' of lesbian movement in Russia; there are photographs representing specific styles and images of such women. These texts are marked by optimism and lightness, as well as a certain excitement. Any association with sexism is missing. Either homosexual female love, or feminism, or any other non-standard manifestation of female individuality does not cause any negative emotions and panic or fear of the contributors to this magazine, which is not characteristic of *Om*: 'Lesbians, just as other women, are very different. They are not looking for sex, they are looking for love' (*Ptyuch*, 1997, No.4).

New Sensuality in the 1990s

In the view of *Om* magazine, the youth cultures of the 1990s have put new, light green and synthetic, colours upon the traditional concepts of the manifestation of sexual feelings. The desire to resuscitate 'live experience', in the light of which the canons created by mankind are only elements of collage, is presented as the main manifestation of this 'new' sensuality: 'The new sensuality is reanimated by way of sticking one's fingers in the socket. The sacrificial breasts of a goddess, given to you on a plate, are begging "eat me!", or ask you the questions of a transvestite "guess whom we belong to! What are we made of!"' (*Om*, Dec. 1996). Together with the manifestation of this new sensuality, a 'sacred attitude' of the youth to fashion has also been changed. Fashion is always in a state of change which is formulated by the youth themselves as an existential question of sorts: 'What am I to wear?' If the old-time romantics, following Mikhail Lermontov, used to say 'In Russia the old fashion is followed by the low-born people' and therefore people who had good taste had to die young, in the youth cultures of the 1990s it is not appropriate to behave in this vein any more. 'The current multi-style fashion took the totalitarian and romantic notions, such as greatness, death, future, out of its sphere' (*Om*, Dec. 1996).

In *Ptyuch* the main elements of the new sensuality are great hedonism, a new cyber-sexuality – 'love with the internet' – and masturbation; the opportunity to get involved even in the most intimate sexual fantasies such as sado-masochism; the desire to discuss openly any 'forbidden' subjects such as fellatio and sex with children. I found a genuine manifesto of sexuality in one of the readers' letters. Addressing his favourite magazine

Ptyuch, a reader is asking to follow traditions of decent, but not puritanical, attitudes to sex:

> Sexuality exists independently of us, it's like electric charges, it penetrates everywhere. Sex is a miracle and, as every miracle, it should be studied and its great power should be demonstrated with gentle enchantment. This power arouses us and throws us into each other's embraces. And what about the world of fashion? People do not look at what one is wearing, they look when one is not wearing anything. (*Ptyuch*, 1996, No.7)

The main principle of great hedonism is 'what I want', not 'what is appropriate'. Pleasures could save you from the main fear of boredom and monotonous sexual orientations. 'This' is so attractive that any devices on your road to sexual pleasure are acceptable. A specific subject for *Ptyuch* is auto-eroticism. The motives of masturbation are present in all publications about the internet and cyber-communities.

Variations on the Subject of Masturbation

> I am 22 years old and I can also tell you something interesting about my sexual experiences ... The cucumber is not only for eating. I was taught to be fastidious about masturbation. But I like the sight of masturbating men ... I understood what the advantages of solo act are: you do not depend on the size of your partner's penis, you control the whole process from start to finish. You should not adjust yourself to your partner ... Now my relationships with men have become normal. I don't treat them only as potential partners. If it doesn't work with my lover, I know that I could always make it with a cucumber. (*Ptyuch*, 1996, No.9)

Masturbation, in comparison to sex between two people, is a real freedom in relation to your partner, it is a liberation from one's yearning for orgasm which is essentially a boring chase for an effective end to sexual contacts: 'It often happens that you quietly hate your boring girlfriend, that you dream about getting rid of her and masturbating somewhere in the corner' (*Ptyuch*, 1997, No.3). The most reliable helper for the effective masturbation is the internet, where the human factor, one's looks and one's feelings do not matter. The sterility of a computer's thinking dominates:

> We are glad again – there is a porno on the internet! Now you can take your favourite notebook and become engrossed in good old masturbation, forgetting about everything else in the world. The unhealthy infantilism of contemporary cyber-punks increases one's attraction to virtual sex. (*Ptyuch*, 1997, No.4)

If there is a threat in this entertainment it is linked to a fledgling new philosophy of those who masturbate, which accompanies masturbation itself: 'A total dystrophy of sexual excitement could begin. The children will cease to be born. A new great age of onanists is coming. A frozen instinct is stylish. The internet needs an army of masturbators' (*Ptyuch*, 1997, No.5). The most obvious advantage of such sex is its complete safety: 'Now if you want to take part in stylish and sterile philosophy, just like everyone else, simply masturbate. Masturbate and the internet will be your kind helper' (*Ptyuch*, 1997, No.6). Talking about a new sensuality in *Ptyuch*, one should not forget about the subject of pleasures which increase adrenaline in your blood, or the search for extreme situations in love. If *Om* pays more attention to cult heroes of the film 'Addicted' (the subject of grunge and heroin punks is presumably closer to its cultural stylists), *Ptyuch* considers the film 'Crash' (director Kronenberg) the most 'cult', which again confirms my guess about the predominantly technocratic version of the discourse in *Ptyuch*.

Certain critics, as well as Kronenberg himself, state that 'Crash' is a film about love. 'Crash' sometimes looks similar to an encyclopaedia of sex: all the types of sexual relations can be found there, from masturbation to lesbian love. The main theme, sexual excitement of the characters when they become witnesses to a car crash or take part in it, is explained by Kronenberg himself thus: 'Nowadays people's attitude to psychological deviations is changing. We have become more tolerant towards extreme forms of sexual behaviour' (*Ptyuch*, 1997, No.3).

The power and attraction of the film 'Crash' is not only in a subtle analysis of, and illustrations to, the notion of perversion. It is also in the search for new unknown forms of sex on the edge based on a fair portion of adrenaline, as well as on sex on the verge of death, and the strong feelings which stem from it:

> One can fully understand new pathological relations between the men and the technical equipment only when he or she tries it on. As any work of art, any car crash is full of energy. In this case I am talking about sexual energy. When love-making reminds us about a car crash, it makes us partake of secret knowledge. This is an attempt to get rid of the main fear of our time, the fear of boredom. (*Ptyuch*, 1997, No.3)

Let me take as an example one of the numerous variations of this 'forbidden' theme. Leaving aside a detailed and lengthy narration of fellatio, I would draw your attention to one detail. Descriptions like that are very close to tabloid press and only the magazine's good taste and a hint of irony allows it to retain its respectable position. However, all these descriptions remind one of something like the manual 'Masturbate! Beginners' Level':

> I do not understand why some girls have a problem with swallowing. I performed the first fellatio when I was still in school. A 17-year-old boy whom I dreamt about for hours became the chosen lucky person ... I bent over, unzipped his trousers and made him have the greatest time in his life ... The most important thing was to start. Before I turned 17 I had swallowed more sperm than school breakfasts. To do fellatio to a man and make his burden lighter is the best way to make him go abusive. Men like this sort of pleasure and stop very reluctantly. My knickers were wet 24 hours a day, 7 days a week ...
> (*Ptyuch*, 1997, No.6)

The Transformation of the Human Body

The image of one's body is usually in the very centre of journalistic discourses about youth sexuality – and consciously so. Regardless of the forms and types of contemporary sexuality, the human body has always been the main participant in such actions. The question is whether it is the body which defines for a human being certain limits of sexual behaviour and sexual pleasure, or whether the body is dictated to about what to do, and how and where to do it. I deliberately emphasize this point. It is obvious that there is no real opposition of the above-named approaches in sexual practices. However, there is a certain struggle among ideologists with regard to what should be taken as a foundation and a basis of sexuality.

The idea of mixed gender directly deals with the problem of the human body. It is with the human body that it fights in the first place, when people are trying to break the limits given to them by nature. It is the human body that is hidden beneath the standardized clothes, it is the human body which is experimented with when someone cuts the hair or puts on make-up. It is the human body which becomes mutilated and therefore defines the boundaries between fear, pain and pleasure. The struggle *with* one's body and the struggle *for* one's body are manifestations of a relationship with power. It is not surprising that many contemporary variations of this theme of shifts in sexuality have influenced our desire to change the state of our bodies. New tendencies, such as the mixture of sexes, ages and nations, produce new perceptions about the mutual relationship between body and spirit, the intellect and the instincts, as related to the notion of sexuality. One of the results is a definite victory of the intellectual search and fantasy over the body which is given to us when we are born. From the main participant in sexual 'parties' our body turns into an experimental base, into a laboratory of transformations. A certain magic is performed on it; it becomes changed, transformed, mocked, argued with.

The theme of *experiments with the masculine body* has been discussed in the pages of *Om*:

> We have a woman already, a boy should be made. He should be cut and stitched back again, reshaped and cut out again. To become someone's husband he has to leave his mother and go nowhere, to roam in this nowhere and belong absolutely to nobody. It goes without saying that any operation (it doesn't matter whether it is performed on a body or on a spirit) does not end without a trace. There are scars which are there to remain. A man's body is newspaper relief, on which a women can read his past. Who could blame her in the desire to hold a real stud in her hands? (*Om*, Oct.–Nov.1996)

Texts devoted to a search for man's body are interesting not only because of their historical details but also because of the special expressions which describe the bodily side of initiations: 'On the surface the procedure of turning a boy into a man looks like this: they are taken to a square to a very big and scary heap of branches and grass. Mad from fear, they hear an angry growl coming from this heap and wet their pants' (*Om*, Oct.–Nov.1996).

This is a description of a soft version of the beginning of a masculine initiation. Now comes a hard version:

> They are left without food and clothes in complete solitude and despair. Male initiators read hypnotic texts about the nothingness of the boys who are poisoned by motherly fluids and have to die. Female initiators put yellow clay on them and make fun of their small penises. They are beaten so that their blood shows, in order to 'open their skin', for three days in a row … Driven to absolute nervous exhaustion they lose their consciousness. The son of a woman has to die in order to raise as a stud. (*Om*, Oct.–Nov. 1996)

The most telling and classic element of the creation of a masculine body is of course circumcision. It is an indispensable element of initiation:

> One's foreskin is essentially nothing else than one's vagina in which the head of one's penis is hidden. To divide the masculine and the feminine, to get rid of divine bisexuality (Gods have both masculine and feminine abilities), to deny one's inherent resemblance to God and become immortal, an eight-day-old boy is given a circumcision (by Jews). (*Om*, Oct.–Nov. 1996)

By contrast, the magazine *Ptyuch* does not carry detailed publications on the subject of initiations. I can refer only to one small quotation taken from readers' letters: 'the orgasm of a circumcised man could not be compared to the orgasm of a non-circumcised man'. In *Ptyuch*'s view, circumcision is yet another technique of sexual pleasure.

The most widespread ways of working with one's body in youth cultures are body piercing and tattooing. Tattoos do not change the shape of the human body, they only add an extra charm to it, emphasizing the significance of certain details. In this traditionally a masculine way of experimenting with the body there have been significant changes: the emphasis has shifted towards the desire to attract a sexual partner. *Ptyuch* suggests an interesting interpretation of the influence of tattoos on the attitude of new Russians to their mobile phones:

> The most popular tattoos are now being drawn on the mobile phones. The majority of customers treat their mobile phones as a natural extension of their bodies. The main drawback of tattoos is that they age together with one's body. The mobile phone, however, is a part of one's body which doesn't age. (*Ptyuch*, 1997, No.7)

The mobile phone is first a symbol and only then a telephone. To the heroes of today it means the same thing as a sword with a handle inlaid with diamonds to a French aristocrat or a walking stick to a dandy from London. Yesterday it seemed a useless luxurious thing; today the mobile phone has taken a respectable place among the powerful phallocratic symbols. People take pride in these things, they readily show them, they write songs about them.

Body piercing (and putting rings through one's body) has also been discussed. For example, in *Om*: 'There are only three reasons to have your body pierced: either you like suffering, or you wish to look like Dennis Rodman or you need additional accessories for your love games' (*Om*, May 1997).

> The interpretation of the meaning of this or that decoration is obtained through the reaction of your real or potential sexual partner (it applies to both men and women). As far as body piercing is concerned: if you have your ear pierced, it impresses only women from the Third World; if you have it in your nose, it impresses female rockers dressed in leather; if you have it in your tongue, the unlimited number of women get impressed and they usually ask you to demonstrate your tongue with a ring on it; a ring in your belly-button mostly attracts men not women; in your nipple – elegant women who like biting (their reaction is 'Oh, it's even more sensitive than my nipples'); a ring in your penis causes reaction mostly among female friends of the women with whom you recently slept. (*Om*, May 1997)

There are also unusual games with masculine bodies. It is make-up applied during the day. The magazine announces its position very resolutely: masculine make-up has nothing to do with perversion:

> Don't forget to put your make-up on! Sensation! In May you have to put your make-up on in order to be a 100 per cent beautiful man. You shouldn't turn your back on us and blame us for perversion. Masculine make-up does not necessarily imply relationships between representatives of the same sex. On the contrary, if your make-up is well applied, it will hide your drawbacks and will emphasize what should be emphasized. (*Om*, June 1997)

> A weather-beaten masculine mouth is simply disgusting. On the contrary, the sexually appealing pink lips are the latest thing in fashion. (*Om*, July–Aug. 1997)

Ptyuch likewise has taken up the theme of make-up: 'Many men like to dress as women. They use green and raspberry colours, their hair-dos remind one of tropical forests after a hurricane, they use heavy make-up on their young faces, they apply artificial birthmarks, brows and lips which illustrate a certain theme' (*Ptyuch*, 1997, No.6).

The way one looks is no longer enough for a precise definition of one's sexual orientation or even of one's real sex. Certain traditionally homosexual motifs, after they had been affected by 'acid',[7] cease to be direct sub-cultural symbols, and they are easily borrowed by and used in other cultural contexts:

> At the end of the 1980s short hair, brushed forward, as it used to be done in ancient Rome and in the 1960s, was a homosexual symbol. In the 1990s the hair à la Caesar has left gay clubs. These hair-dos are worn by 'normal' men across the globe, and these men are not worried in the slightest that they could be mistaken for gays. (*Om*, Oct.–Nov. 1996)

The rave culture which takes the most impressive space in the youth practices of the 1990s is a triumph of synthetics, 'acid' and unisex. This acid not only affects music: it also takes part in the construction of the body of a true raver.

> The narrow eyes of Ghenghis Khan look like a remote and endless horizon ... 'Boiled' hair is just like a washing-up mop. A face with the colour of a carrot with bright red lips as a cave ... a large number of small rings with magic symbols on them which cover practically all the fingers. The renovation should be radical. The 'flying' lines of the house style will make you more impressive, they will attract new admirers and produce fans. (*Om*, July–Aug. 1997)

The light green synthetics has found a new free niche: the eyes. They could not be tattooed or have a ring put through them, but one can change their colour and make them look like the eyes of a wolf:

> You meditate at a discothèque, you are after the energy for your personal biological field and the trance sucks you in. And here on the brink of ecstasy, your eyes begin to burn with a hellish green light in the pink rays of the discothèque! The explanation of this miracle is given by the ophthalmology at the end of the second millennium: in your eyes you have extremely original contact lenses which are noticeable only in the light of a discothèque or in a bright moonlight. Have you ever seen the eyes of a wolf, closely and in the dark? No! Good for you! But these cold lights will burn in your eyes if you are not afraid of being original. Believe me, today you will be the only one but tomorrow there will be more of such wolves at fashionable parties. (*Om*, Dec. 1996)

Recently self-mutilation has become one of the most extreme manifestations of experiments with the human body. Wounds and scars on one's body are not always an imitation: sometimes they are real. This passion has its examples in history. For instance, it was very fashionable to imitate marks left by the rope or by the guillotine on one's neck at the time of the French Revolution: this was especially popular among excited female aristocrats. Today's trend has mostly been influenced by the cult of self-mutilation or suicide, which stems from Kurt Kobain (of the band 'Nirvana'). This trend is equally similar to the cult of ugliness, of the open cynicism towards 'proper' beauty and American propaganda of the 'healthy way of life'. Britain is considered the 'motherland' of the extravagant fashion of self-mutilation.

The modification of female bodies has also been discussed in the magazines. Women's desire to experiment with their bodies is directly linked to the flourishing of sins at the end of the century and a natural desire on the part of women to be victims, with their masochistic thirst to draw blood:

> At the turn of a century sins really flourish. Human beings begin to change their bodies. Any transformations of their bodies, even the ugly ones, provoke the great interest of potential sexual partners. The most trivial modification of one's body is body-piercing. If one does body-piercing, it usually enhances one's sexual status, but very often it is simply an element of fashion … It is mostly women who suffer from the virus of modification. Their desire to go through an operation is mostly explained by their syndrome of suffering, and also by their passion to be unique. The biological nature of women makes them

experience pain three times more, on average, than men. It is not a problem for them to draw their own blood. Those men who like to modify their bodies are mostly homosexuals. The modification of the human body is usually performed with the only purpose, which is sexual. This is the most progressive way to express your individuality. (*Om*, April 1997)

The tattoo for females is somewhat more important than for men. It is also a proof of their inclination to exhibitionism. There is an interesting sketch in *Ptyuch* magazine about women's tattoos. An article about a series of work by Yurii Balashov is very similar to the idea of hidden female exhibitionism which, in its turn, expects an adequate reaction from the observer–voyeur: 'A series of works about eternity called "Lono" [vagina] consists of picturesque vaginas embellished by strangely looking tattoos each of which is dedicated to a well-known poet or musician' (*Ptyuch*, 1997, No.6).

One of the characteristic features of the discourse in *Om* is an open sexism which is demonstrated in the context of Russian interpretation of the trend for unisex and androgyny. Let us refer to an example which consists of quotations taken from an interview of the editor-in-chief of the magazine, Igor Grigor'ev, with a popular journalist Otar Kushanashvili:

> *About women:* 'Khakamada simply suffers as a woman because she doesn't have a strong man next to her ... As a stud, I am convinced that as a women she feels as if she is in deep shit. I am not even talking about the extremist version of the faction "Russian women" such as Yekaterina Lakhova. The shortage of fellatios which they had in their lives is written all over their faces ... What do you think about women who scream at concerts? Yeh, they scream, the bitches ...'

> *About the magazine:* 'What is *Om*, what is Grigor'ev? Penis, boobs, add some blood, here's your magazine.'

> *About homosexuals:* 'Homos, poofs – fuck them. They are feeble, they are weak ... He was a pure Romanian homosexual ... He was dressed in a silly fur coat, just like those poofs do, and I wanted to hit him over the head immediately. If you see a man who speaks affectedly, hit him over his head, you won't make a mistake. I wanted to tell him "Would you like to suck my dick?"' (*Om*, May 1997)

Rovesnik

I would like to conduct separately the analysis of the texts in the magazines *Rovesnik*, *Shestnadtsat* ('16') and the supplement for women called *Shtuchka*. This is because the discourse in these magazines is significantly different from the discourse in *Om* and *Ptyuch*, as far as their cultural, thematic and linguistic aspects are concerned.

Homosexuality and Other 'Perversions'

'Every man turns into a woman for seven days in his life.'[8] It is not by chance that I start my analysis with this quotation. It characterizes very well the whole discourse of this magazine about this form of sexuality. Although the obvious homophobia is missing from this magazine, the talk about this subject does not go down very well.

For the few stories about homosexuality and homosexuals, a narrative approach is taken. Various stories are described by recourse to verbs and moral assessments. There are hardly any abstract thoughts and images. After the foregoing analysis of sexual discourses in the other magazines, it is striking that the contributors to *Rovesnik* do not deliberate on the subject of the general and the specific in homosexuality and bisexuality, they do not try to find out what is so special about the fashion for unisex. All these varieties are confined to the same space, namely that of unconventional sexual orientation. The examples which are used by the contributors to *Rovesnik* to illustrate such subjects are either unassuming stories about American Indians ('16', 1996, No.10; '16', 1996, No.4), or about strange French lesbians: 'She looks like a typical French woman, yet she's not the same as all her friends. She has a female lover' (*Rovesnik*, 1997, No.7), or about famous pop singers, actors and sports people:

> Elton John honestly and sincerely confessed to the world about his unconventional sexual orientation. It was a bold move which brought not shame but respect to the singer. Especially because Elton John's profession is not homosexuality, it's singing. ('16', 1996, No.7)

> Everybody has thought at one point that bisexuality might happen to him or her, but many people keep silent about it. However, a person who declares that he or she has never tried bisexuality or homosexuality is simply lying. (*Rovesnik*, 1997, No.3)

The increase in the popularity of this trend in show business has a simple explanation:

> The scale of this new movement is most striking. Rock stars are not lonely in their bisexuality any more, they have now loads of emulators. The fashion for bisexuality is swiftly moving along the road of commercialization: the owners of hotels and bars offer bi-service, Calvin Klein produces fragrance with a new aroma for men and women. Heterosexuality looks banal, homosexuality is despised, hence one has to put one's stakes on bisexuality. ('16', 1996, No.4)

We could find only one note on this subject under the rubric, 'Details from Sasha' (a mature and experienced man gives advice to women), and this note is not about a star:

'Dear Sasha, please help! I do not know what to do! I have taken a liking to a boy but recently I have found out that he is homosexual.' Here is Sasha's response: 'A female friend of mine thinks that it is impossible to find a better friend for a woman than a male homosexual. The friendship between a man and a women is a very subtle matter; such friendship is precious and what often gets in its way is sex'. (*Shtuchka*, 1997, No.5)

A strange article about the role of buttocks in history could be seen as a manifestation of hidden homosexuality. Perhaps it has become possible for us to find hints at homosexuality here only after having studied the bohemian texts in *Om*:

The human being differs from the monkey by his or her buttocks. One's behind is trying to return to itself the old status, lost in time. Buttocks used to be originally a symbol of love. Look into any manual of anatomy and compare the real heart with its symbol. Nothing in common, is there? Who was that censor who decided to change one's behind into a heart? It is for certain that every man likes the sight of female behinds but very rarely admits to it, unless he is a bully. What about women? Opinion polls show that for them male behinds are the most sexual part of a male's body, but they also prefer to keep silent about it, pretending that they are mostly interested in men's shoulders. ('16', 1996, No.7)

A very small part of the magazine is devoted to the description of various sins linked to sexual deviations. One article is devoted to passionate love between older men and little girls. Another article is devoted to debauchery in Ancient Rome. Debauchery and sins belong to the ancient times:

Nymphomania is an example of illness and nastiness, but not love ... Although the novel *Lolita* by Nabokov is brilliantly written, it cannot justify such a perversion. However, such people call their pathological passion 'love' and psychologists believe that they are sincere. ('16', 1996, No.8)

Valeria Messalina, the wife of the Roman Emperor Claudius, was famous for being the most depraved first lady in the history of mankind. The debauchery was normal for aristocrats, chastity was considered a sign of decline, and lust played the role of ideology and was seen as a sign of the faithfulness to the emperor. ('16', 1996, No.8)

There are stories about prostitution in this magazine, but to demonstrate this type of sexual deviation, it refers only to Western countries, such as Germany, France and the United States.

Basic Sexual Education

The majority of the articles could be called 'basic sexual education for beginners' or 'how to make sure you lead a sexual life and remain a well-to-do virgin'. Unlike the reprints from Western magazines referred to above, the majority of articles from this series are from the pens of members of the editorial board. The following are a number of examples that appeared under the rubric 'Sex Without Fear'.

'How to make him put the condom on?' ('16', 1996, No.10). In this article one can find a detailed description of the proper tactic of behaviour with a young man so that he does not become scared and does not think that this is an experienced woman in front of him, but he will get maximum pleasure from this encounter. There is also an article called 'The miracle of the condom', and a number of photographs treating the subject of 'The condoms of our parents' ('16', 1997, No.4).

Another article, entitled 'Stop the intercourse and you'll enjoy it', is about a method which does not require expense, namely about how to stop sexual intercourse, about the advantages and drawbacks of such methods ('16', 1996, No.8). 'Pieces of advice to young ladies' is, on the one hand, a hymn to virginity as the most significant and the only real value to any woman. On the other hand, however, these pieces of advice are very provocative because all women's efforts are supposed to be directed at conquering men sexually.

'Is it worth keeping your virginity?' The first advice is: Don't be in a hurry, choose the 'right' person. Advice number two: Friendship first, sex second. Advice number three: Let it be beautiful. Advice number four: The best sex is safe sex: 'And the most beautiful thing is to find a true love and to give to this man your very special gift, your virginity' (*Shtuchka*, 1997, No.5).

'Shall I have sex or not?' It is suggested that this sacred question should to be solved by young men and women themselves. However, they are reminded that, while solving this problem, one should remember that: 'The success of every business depends on how it begins ... It is practically impossible to climb to the seventh heaven of love without educating your feelings, without preliminary training. Any man simply has to go through this because it is him who introduces a woman to the world of sex' ('16', 1996, No.10).

The making of female sexuality is related to the experience of women's communications with men. Here the magazine openly demonstrates a heterosexual orientation. In its articles there is a clear distinction between sex and love. Sex is a physiological attraction which is characterized by obsession, therefore it should be repressed. The most proper thing to do is to restrict yourself and concentrate on 'true' feelings:

> Maybe it is difficult for you to restrict yourself and you want to have sex desperately? Sex with a guy is not a recipe for love. Sex is a physical act, and love is an emotional state. If there is no love, it doesn't matter whether you want love to be there or not – having sex will not change anything. On the other hand, if love exists already and this a mutual love, then sex as well as the lack of it will not be able to change your and your lover's feelings. ('16', 1996, No.4)

'You, your guy and your sex'. This article gives advice on how to reject a guy properly if he is insisting on sex and his girl simply wants to remain his girl: 'Tell him that you are not ready for sex yet. If once you were brave enough to say a firm and calm no, later on you will learn to give longer speeches, aimed at defending your dignity and your views of life. Try and you will succeed' (*Rovesnik*, 1997, No.5).

There is also advice for those who have already entered the world of sex for this or that reason. For example, there is a publication in the magazine in which sexologists strongly recommend to the new couples not to remain silent when they make love:

> 'Dear, don't be silent!' You are in bed with your lover, not on a job interview. The majority of men like it when their partners do not hold their emotions back. You don't have to worry what sounds to make, what words to utter. You can say anything you want to say from muffled sounds of a touchy person to the wild victorious shouts of a cowgirl. Everything depends on your temperament and character. Your partner will get excited by any sound. ('16', 1996, No.8)

'A piece of advice to a young womanizer, or the manual for a beginning Casanova.' This article talks about the technology of womanizing which, according to its authors, should avoid elementary mistakes and help to be versatile:

> A man takes a look at his object from head to toe, fixing his gaze at various parts, then sits next to her, offers her a cocktail and puts his arm around her waist, 'I like your T-shirt, how about making love?' There is an example of how one shouldn't behave ... Look at her from head to toe, look at anything you like. When she notices you, look directly into her eyes ... rudeness doesn't help the relationship, whereas tenderness and softness diminishes a woman's resistance.

'Your hair is so beautiful.' Touch her neck. The fear of confessing your physical attraction is one of the forms of impotence. If you feel that this is the right moment to start with the last stage of seduction, look into her eyes, put your confident and soothing arm around her waist and think of a pretext to stay in the room longer ... (*Rovesnik*, 1996, No.10)

And finally, some practical advice from a star (the advice by Boy George, the British pop singer): 'Make love as often as you can. It's advisable that your partner is a person who you really like. No "lip service" please. Be restless, turn around constantly, you will lose lots of calories and improve your sensation!' ('16', 1996, No.4). A desperate letter by a young admirer, a *Rovesnik* reader, is a response to such advice. This letter was published under a shocking title 'I took the bull by the horns and tore her knickers off':

I am 18, and this is the best time for sex, as specialists unanimously suggest. If one is to believe these specialists I need only ten minutes after my orgasm to recover and be ready for further feats. What would we do without science! It is a consolation to know that according to the latest scientific discoveries, women have to be mad about me! Why is it then, that I am crap in bed? (*Rovesnik*, 1997, No.5)

Many publications in *Rovesnik* magazine are devoted to various classifications of the types of boys and girls. The principle of these classifications is sexual quality:

Specially for a woman who is looking for a male sexual partner

Read and guess which type is your partner – a serious political and social problem.
Pretenders: they have sex to impress their friends. A smoothy liar: when having sex he is trying to prove to himself and to people around him that he is a real man. Womanizers: they don't like to woo you, they need sex straight away because they cannot think about other relationships between men and women. Voluptuary: their favourite expression is 'relax and enjoy'. The possessive type: they are hardened egoists. If a woman is seeing him, she belongs to him with all her possessions. The possessive type doesn't know the word no. The best thing is to break up with such a type immediately. You are not his slave and you don't have to agree to everything he suggests. (*Rovesnik*, 1997, No. 3)

Specially for a guy who is looking for a female sexual partner

What should a partner of a hero look like? Not every woman is worthy of our company and not every woman who looks like the one who is worthy is not necessarily worthy. The silly type: a very good and useful woman; keep her in reserve in case of unforeseen circumstances, but you shouldn't be friends with her. The moron: almost an ideal thing, especially if she is beautiful. The calculating and careful type: mercifully such types do not walk along our street and if they did by pure chance they would start testing all aborigines which we will never pass. Her mother's daughter: it is clinical and hopeless; her attractive appearance should not deceive you. The brainy one: you can prove to her that all her knowledge is taken from TV programmes and she doesn't know anything about real life, but this will take too much time. The beauty who's mad about money: it wouldn't be a problem if she was mad about you as well, but usually this is not the case. (*Shtuchka*, 1997, No.6)

The first thing that strikes one is that adolescents are offered an openly instrumental approach to the choice of partner. The comparison of these classifications could serve as a good illustration to sexism in its soft version and 'snootiness' to women, on the one hand; on the other hand, it could testify to a deep conviction about the leading role of men in this choice. Gentle and pleasing attributes are used here to characterize men, whereas superficial attributes are used here to characterize women.

Additional illustrations relate to one type: a vamp, a treacherous seducer and a bitch. This attraction has a simple explanation. The contributors insist that such women are the main danger to any man because they are after their souls, bodies and wallets. The main target for such bitches is a wealthy man with a good 'pedigree' and their main concern is a profitable marriage. Because there are so many of them these days they are beginning to become a real threat. The danger comes only from women, and men, by contrast, should be taught how to seduce better and more effectively.

Seducers and bitches

When she meets a man of her whimsical dreams she goes after him like a tank. Nobody can stop her. She is a tornado woman, an embodiment of romantic dreams of silly women, about limitless love. To be precise, it's love out of all proportion. Although she looks like a schizophrenic, she will never fall in love with a penniless guy. It is extremely important from her point of view to have a tall, broad shouldered handsome 'object'. However, a wealthy 'dog' will also do fine. ('16', 1996, No.10)

How does one recognize a vamp?

She hasn't got a gun in her hand but she's not harmless. She looks gentle and fragile but actually she's stronger than steel. ... She is not the woman who doesn't hide her aggression and wages an open and honest war, the way men do. Clever men are not afraid of such amazons any more. Those who wear silk underwear instead of a pistol are much more dangerous. ... A girl with an angelic smile.

A number of rules for a *femme fatale* follow. The lack of psychological complexes is most important:

You have knees like a chicken? Do not try to hide this treasure! A short dress with flowers on it is just what you need. Let your man think that you are so fragile, unpredictable and controversial. Men like to feel that they are strong so much! You have a naive face with a nose like a potato? It's a treasure and do not apply make-up as if you are Elizabeth Taylor. And if you will try your best not to say anything clever in his presence, if you only try to smile and look at him with your eyes wide open, then you might pass yourself off as an attractive, silly woman. You have to combine incompatible things: be helpless and strong, naive, clever, innocent and corrupt. ('16', 1996, No.7)

And finally there is important advice by the 'superior bitch' addressed to the 'beginner bitches':

Are you not tired of listening to these well-bred women? You are you. The only one, the unique. The first rule of the beginner bitch: hit him on the nose by the most memorable fragrance. That will knock him off his feet! Secondly, never listen to anyone. You should only talk yourself. Thirdly, don't let those who are around you to look down upon you: keep your eyes half-closed and look at all these stupid cretins, at their belly button or below their waist ... You should wear dark glasses all the time, or better, Ray-Bans. (*Shtuchka*, 1997, No.6)

Conclusions

Although not all aspects of the presentation of sexuality are as directly comparable as appears in Table 2, it may be useful to attempt to bring together the key elements of journalistic sexual discourse in such a way.

Every discourse is formed by somebody (contributors, sources, references), for somebody (the target audience), relying on the knowledge and intuitive concept about the level of competence of the audience, about something (the subject and its aspects), in a certain way (by recourse to certain means, technologies and associations), using the initiator's own language understood by the audience, with a certain aim (target, concept), appealing to significant authorities in this virtual society. According to this

TABLE 2

CONCEPTS AND SOCIOCULTURAL MODELS OF SEXUALITY IN THE MAGAZINES *OM, PTYUCH* AND *ROVESNIK*

Main parameters of sexual and gender discourse in journalistic publications	Om	Ptyuch	Magazines of the *Rovesnik* series
1. The leading social-cultural type	Aristocratically bohemian homosexual	Bisexual–masturbator	Heterosexual with developed, socially acceptable sexual inclinations
2. Social status of the main character in journalistic publications	Wealthy bohemian group, cultural underground movement in Russian capital cities, provincial elite	Clubbing youth, DJs, their admirers, those who go to elite rave discos	Teenagers on the brink of active sexual life, disco-goers, fans of pop music
3. Sexual (and gender) orientation of the magazines	Homosexuality of the masculine type, sexism, misogyny	Bisexuality, lack of sexism and homophobia, masculine and feminine roles are mixed	Heterosexuality, sexism, traditionally patriarchal concepts of masculinity and femininity
4. Sexual 'technologies' – ways to experience new sexual sensations	Intellectual search for 'true' love without any concern for its gender side. Experiments with 'high' drugs	Masturbation and sex on the verge of death. Obtaining pleasures of the highest quality by recourse to adrenaline-producing experiments in any form	Awareness of the rules of normal, effective and safe sex, and of your partner's psychology
5. The technique of promoting (creating) your type	Sacred texts, manifestos, appeals, myths, practical jokes, magazine performances	Difficult, in both form and content; texts: tales, true stories, confessions	Sexual education – advice, recommendations, taboos and instructions
6. The language of the publications on sexuality	Snobbish use of obscenities, provocative statements about untraditional love-making, shocking tactics	English words; relishing the most minute details of one's progress to orgasm, shocking words and expressions	Correct literary language, 'normal' vocabulary. Simplified way of communication.
7. Concepts of sexuality (its philosophy and ideology)	Search for post-homosexual concepts, laddism, fight against the over-simplification of any symbols and their use as clichés	Search for a new concept of technocratic sex (the internet and I)	Propaganda of 'normal' and healthy sex in the family and safe sex before the marriage
8. Cult sexual symbols, significant cultural authorities	Oscar Wilde, Marilyn Monroe, the film 'Addicted', the music of Nirvana and Oasis	House music, the film 'Crash'	Advice by experienced friends, sexologists, psychologists, rock and pop stars
9. The 'Motherland' of a new sexual experience	Britain	Britain and Russia	USA
10. Goals (targets) of sexual discourse	Enlightenment, progress to Western freedoms and democracies	Relaxation, rest, liberation	Basic sexual education for adolescents
11. Sexual anti-type	Heterosexual philistine, pop music, feminists	Homophobe, sexist	All untraditional sexual types

logic I have defined the parameters of discourses about sexuality which I used as a foundation for Table 2.

As can be seen, therefore, there are common elements of sexual and gender discourses in *Om* and *Ptyuch*. These may be summmmarized as:

- The majority of articles in these two magazines, directly or obliquely, deal with the problem of sexuality. Many of them are triggered by the idea of the end of the millennium as a harbinger of cynicism.

- Sexual globalization, via the development of sex industry on a global scale, is presented as a basis for the merger of nations.

- The subject of homosexuality has turned into a popular product put out by show business and pleasure industries. *Om* is mostly oriented toward the search for a new concept of homosexuality, whereas *Ptyuch* is mostly preoccupied with the fight against the concept of homosexuals as ill and queer. The majority of articles in *Om* deal with bohemian and aristocratic homosexual symbols. *Ptyuch* demonstrates a more democratic and versatile gallery of homosexuals. *Om* is chiefly talking about the masculine version of homosexuality, whereas *Ptyuch* is oriented towards bi-sexuality and multi-sexuality (from homo-eroticism to auto-eroticism).

There remain, however, specific elements to the discourse in each magazine. *Om* presents the necessary destruction of moral taboos as a healthy cynicism, which includes liberation from the limits of gender, and also mockery of this liberation. *Ptyuch* presents the liberation of the burden of moral duties as an innocent, exciting cynicism and a joyful provocation. This exciting cynicism is a mocking attitude to American values. The joyful provocation is the only remedy for boredom. *Om* demonstrates a more ideologically loaded and conceptual approach to the idea of the mixture of accents on gender and the mixture of the sexes. For *Om*, unisex is a subject for discussion; *Ptyuch* suggests a total 'unisexualization'. The contributors to *Om* and *Ptyuch* treat the sources of new sensuality and new sexuality differently. For *Om*, this source is in the reanimation of the 'live' experience, in which the elements of old canons of sexuality are used as collage. The new sensuality in *Ptyuch* is linked to the 'great' hedonism, which will save us from boredom and monotonous sexual orientation. *Ptyuch* is looking for something 'below the surface' in everything, in what is not degraded to the level of pop, in everything generally original. *Om* turns this originality into clichés by putting the 'usual' ('pop') things through a shining prism. This allows one 'to turn your activity into a subject of common interest within the limits of a necessary segment of the audience' (from readers' letters). The underground movement lives according to the laws of the market. For the discourse about sexuality in *Om* the following features can be deemed characteristic: homosexuality, laddism (the masculine version of homosexuality), sexism and bohemian lifestyle. For *Ptyuch* it is bisexuality, multi-sexuality, the unisexuality of ravers in nightclubs, anti-sexism and democracy. *Rovesnik* magazine has a a quite different discourse of sexuality which may be summarized thus:

- The majority of publications devoted to sexuality would not be disapproved of by parents; the language of their publications is that of teachers and preachers.

- The existence of marginal sexual inclinations is inferred only through articles about Ancient history or those worlds which are far away from us.

- The magazine demonstrates a blatantly heterosexual orientation without obvious signs of homophobia but with certain elements of sexism.

- The sexual discourse of the magazine is fairly controversial. On the one hand sins are evil, on the other hand there is advice to the 'beginner bitches' and 'seducers'.

- The overwhelming majority of aarticles are translations, mostly from American sources. There are too many classifications and tests. All types of advice are united into the 'patriarchal manifesto': the girl's aim is not to be abused, the boy's aim is to reach his goal.

- All types of advice are given by older and experienced adults. There is a transmission of sexual values of the traditional society modelled on the American middle class. In their list of recommended videos there are no films with sexual scenes.

- The main fear which accompanies the process of having sex is not illness, it is pregnancy.

This study devoted to the problems of sexuality and new cultural trends linked to these problems has confirmed the hypothesis about the leading role of these ideas in the discourses of youth publications. One of the possible interpretations is: the struggle for 'sexual orientation' (in its broad sense) of young people is a struggle for power over their minds. The preliminary analysis of the texts has shown that there is a certain common cultural and social space within which parameters of such discourses could be placed:

- Homo – heterosexual continuum

- Homo-mania and homophobia (homo-chauvinism)

- Defined gender – mixed or shifted gender
- Sexism (misogyny) – antisexism
- The principle of sexual pleasure as health – the principle of sexual pleasure as illness
- Traditional (socially acceptable) sex – shocking sex
- Sex on the edge (catastrophic sex) – healthy sex
- Sex in the family (the birth of children) – sex between partners, not linked to the idea of procreation
- Sexual attraction attached to a certain gender (via the demonstration of masculinity or femininity) – sexual attraction without any certain attachment to a particular gender
- Sexomania (hypersexuality, exhibitionism, voyeurism) – sexophobia (asexuality, latent sex)
- Auto-eroticism (masturbation, sex with toys or special equipment) – sex with a partner

Normal Sex – Abnormal Sex

In this field the struggle between the ideologists of these magazines for their audience is unfolding. For the time being these discourses are not seriously competing with each other and their competition is not very apparent. It can be assumed that the market for youth magazines will expand. For example, *Rovesnik* magazine has recently had a powerful double, *Detki* magazine (this title is chosen not by chance: the association with the popular film 'Kids' is bound to arise instantly), which is positioned, according to its first issue, as a magazine for the physically and morally healthy 'new' Russian youth, modelled after the 'next' American generation. This is a Russian version of a politically-correct youth that leads a healthy lifestyle. The *Ptyuch* magazine has *Ai-da* magazine as a competitor, devoted to stories from the lives of Russian pop stars. The magazines *Cosmo* and *Playboy* have begun to invade the youth space. The constant and detailed study of the discourses of youth magazines helps us to become part of that cultural and informational universe which forms the attitudes and models of sexuality, as well as gender roles of adolescents and youth.

Translated by Andrei Rogachevsky,
University of Glasgow

NOTES

1. A course of my lectures entitled the 'Youth Culture and Sub Culture' is in preparation for publication in the series 'Specialized courses in sociological education'. (This project is supported financially by the Programme of the European Union TEMPUS/TACIS, Project JEP 08517-94).

2. See, for example, the classification of sexual behaviour in the USSR and the concepts of its citizens about sexuality in I.S. Kon, *Seksual'naya kul'tura v Rossii* (Moscow: OGI, 1997), pp.117–18.

3. Every list in each magazine consists of 50 ideas. I have chosen only those which are linked to the promotion of new gender and sexual trends. I reproduce these ideas word by word. Similar ideas are quoted for the comparison.

4. It is significant how this magazine treats British and American cultural experiences. If we are to characterize this distinction as a whole, *Om* magazine could be called pro-British and anti-American.

5. He is talking about Soviet ideology in which the notion of class completely encompassed the notions of man and woman which naturally affected the Soviet fashion industry, which was emphatically a-sexual and beyond sex.

6. Irina Saltykova, in her video tape 'These Little Eyes', earnestly demonstrates to the audience the whole classical sado-masochistic repertoire. The female duet, 'The Vice Squad', imitates lesbian love. The harmless and hopelessly heterosexual pop singer Alexander Ukupnik pretends that he is a transvestite. Konstantin Kinchev, the famous leader of the rock group 'Alisa', still an idol for his fans, wears brown panty-hose, just as Marilyn Manson.

7. The notion of acid comes from contemporary DJ music.

8. This is the heading of an article about the structure of feminine and masculine brains: see '16', 1996, No. 8.

Notes on Contributors

Chris Corrin is Reader in Politics at the University of Glasgow. She has worked for many years with women's groups in Central and Eastern Europe and continues to be involved with women's politics across 'Europe' particularly on issues of violence against women and women's political participation. Her publications include *Superwomen and the Double Burden* (1992); *Magyar Women: Hungarian Women's Lives 1960s–1990s* (1994); *Women in a Violent World: Feminist Analyses and Resistance* (1996) and *Feminist Perspectives on Politics* (1999).

Milica Antić Gaber is a junior lecturer at the Sociology Department, Faculty of Arts, University of Ljubljana, where she also teaches Women's Studies. She was a member of Council of Europe's Group of Experts for Mainstreaming Equality Between Women and Men, and a co-founder of the editorial collective of the first women's review *Delta* in Slovenia, and of the interdisciplinary postgraduate study of feminist theory at the University of Ljubljana. She recently published *Women in Parliament: The Elements Influencing their Representation*. She would like to thank Mateja Mrak Thorne for her help with the translation of this contribution.

Delina Fico is a founding member of the 'Refleksione' women's association and from 1994 until 1997 served as Coordinator of the Women's Centre in Tirana. She taught for four years at Tirana University and later served as a programme officer in the Ministry of Foreign Affairs. She enrolled on a Master of Science course in the Nonprofit Management Programme, New School University, New York and graduated in May 1999.

Urszula Nowakowska is founder and director, since 1995, of the Women's Rights Centre (a non-profit-making NGO), having previously been secretary to the Constitutional Committee, Polish Parliament, Sejm Chancellery. She has held a Congressional Fellowship on Women and Public Policy, Washington, DC, and a fellowship at the Center for Reproductive Law and Policy in New York and in 1994 participated in the Global Leadership Institute, Rutgers University, New Jersey. She has published widely in Polish and English with articles on sexual harassment, division of work between women and men and a legal manual on domestic violence and divorce, and for women's rights in the labour market and chapters in the Women's Legal Status report. She has contributed to Tanya Renne (ed.), *Ana's Land: Sisterhood in Eastern Europe* (Oxford, 1997).

Tatyana Kotzeva is Associate Professor at South West University, Blagoevgrad, Bulgaria, where she has taught introductory sociology and Gender Sociology. She has coordinated and directed many research and social projects on women's identity, women's professional promotion, women's unemployment and child support in the case of separated parents. Her interests are also in the areas of feminist theories and methodologies. She is also an activist in the NGO sector including the Bulgarian Association of Women. Her recent publications include *Bulgarian Women: Traditional Images and Changing Realities* (Pernik: Krakra, 1994).

Elena Omel'chenko is director of the interdisciplinary research centre 'Region' at Ul'yanovsk State University, Russia, and honorary research fellow of Centre for Russian and East European Studies, University of Birmingham. She has researched and published widely in the area of contemporary society and culture in Russia. Her current research interests are in youth and violence and discourses of youth, gender and sexuality.

Select Bibliography

Amnesty International (1988), *Appeal Cases*, March/April, 88:7.

B.a.B.e. (1998), *B.a.B.e. update*, July–December 1998, 6th issue, p.1.

Bhabha, H. (1994), *The Location of Culture*, London: Routledge.

Bhattacharyya, G. (1994), 'Who Fancies Pakis?', in S. Ledger, J. McDonagh and J. Spencer, (eds.), *Political Gender (Texts and Contexts)*, Hemel Hemstead: Harvester Wheatsheaf .

Boric, R. (1996), 'Croatia:Three Years After', in Corrin (ed.) (1996), pp.135–52.

Boric, R. (1995), 'The Oasis', *New Internationalist*, London, Aug., pp.12–13.

Brah, A. (1996), *Cartographies of Diaspora: Contesting Identities*, London and New York: Routledge.

Bresheeth, H. and N. Yuval-Davis (1991), *The Gulf War and the New World Order*, London: Zed Books.

Bridger, S., Kay, R. and K. Pinnick (eds.) (1996), *No More Heroines: Russia, Women and the Market*, London: Routledge.

Brownmiller, S. (1976), *Against our Will: Men, Women and Rape*, Harmondsworth: Penguin.

Bryson, V. (1992), *Feminist Political Theory*, London: Macmillan.

Buckley, M. (ed.) (1997), *Post-Soviet Women: From the Baltic to Central Asia*, Cambridge: Cambridge University Press.

Bunch, C. (1997), 'The Intolerable Status Quo: Violence Against Women and Girls', in *The Progress of Nations*, New York: UNICEF.

Charlesworth, H. (1994), 'What are "Women's International Human Rights"?' in R. Cook (ed.), *Human Rights of Women:National and International Perspective*, Philadelphia, PA: University of Pennsylvania Press, pp.58–84 .

Chatterjee, P. (1989), 'The Nationalist Resolution of the Women's Question', in Kum-Kum Sangari and Sudesh Vaid (eds.), *Recasting Women: Essays in Colonial History*, New Delhi: Kali for Women.

Connors, J. (1989), *Violence Against Women in the Family*, New York: United Nations Office.

Coole, D. (1994), *Women in Political Theory*, Hemel Hemstead: Harvester Wheatsheaf.

Corrin, C. (ed.) (1992), *Superwomen and the Double Burden: Women's Experiences of Change in Central and Eastern Europe and the Former Soviet Union*, London: Scarlet Press.

Corrin, C. (1994), *Magyar Women: Hungarian Women's Lives 1960s to 1990s*, Basingstoke: Macmillan.

Corrin, C. (1998), 'Engendering Citizenship: Feminist Resistance to Male Violence in "Europe"', in V. Ferreira, *et al.* (eds.), *Shifting Bonds, Shifting Bounds: Women Mobility and Citizenship in Europe*, pp.107–24.

Corrin, C. (1999), *Feminist Perspectives on Politics*, London: Pearson Education.

Corrin, C. (ed.) (1996), *Women in a Violent World: Feminist Analyses and Resistance across 'Europe'*, Edinburgh: Edinburgh University Press.

Daily Republika, Daily Slovenec, Slovene Newspapers.

Darcy, Robert, Welch, Susan and Janet Clark (1994), *Women, Elections and Representation*, Lincolnm, NE and London: University of Nebraska Press.

De Lauretis, T. (1987), *Technologies of Gender*, Bloomington, IN: Indiana University Press.

De Stoop, C. (1994), 'They are so Sweet, Sir', in International Organization for Migration (1995), *Trafficking and Prostitution: The Growing Exploitation of Migrant Women from Central and Eastern Europe*, Budapest: Migration Information Programme.

Deimel, J. (1998), Bewegte Zeiten. Frauen in Bulgarien Gestern und Heute', dissertation, Munich: LDV-Verlag.

Einhorn, B. (1993), *Cinderella Goes to Market: Citizenship, Gender, and Women's Movements in East Women's Experience of Change in Central and Eastern Europe and the Central Europe*, London: Verso.

Election Regulations (1992), The Official Gazette of the Republic of Slovenia, Ljubljana.

Enloe, C. (1993), *The Morning After: Sexual Politics at the end of the Cold War*, Berkeley, CA: University of California Press.

Estell, J. (ed.) (1989), *The Nonprofit Sector in International Perspective: Studies in Comparative Culture and Policy*, Oxford: Oxford University Press.

Ferreira, V. *et al.* (eds.) (1998) *Shifting Bonds, Shifting Bounds: Women Mobility and Citizenship in Europe*, Oeiras, Portugal: Celta Editora.

Fico, D. (1993), *Violence Against Women in Central and Eastern Europe* (Albania country report), Prague: Helsinki Citizens Assembly 8.

Funk, N. and M. Mueller (eds.) (1993), *Gender Politics and Post-Communism: Reflections from Eastern Europe and the Former Soviet Union*, London: Routledge.

Gellner, E. (1994), *Encounters with Nationalism*, Oxford: Blackwell.

Grossberg, L. (1997), 'Identity and Cultural Studies – Is That All There Is?', in Hall and du Gay (eds.) (1997).

Haavio-Mannila, E. *et al.* (1985), *Unfinished Democracy: Women in Nordic Politics*, Oxford: Pergamon .

Haavio-Mannila, E. (1981), 'Finland', in Lovenduski and Hills (eds.), *The Politics of Second Electorate*, London: Routledge & Kegan Paul.

Hall, P.D. (1994), 'Historical Perspectives on Nonprofit Organisations', in the *Jossey-Bass Handbook of Nonprofit Leadership and Management*, San Francisco, CA: Jossey-Bass Publishers.

Hall, S. (1997), 'Who Needs "Identity"?', in S. Hall and P. du Gay (eds.), *Questions of Cultural Identity*, London: Sage.

Havel, V. (1985), *The Power of the Powerless*, New York: Armonk.

Heinan, J. (1995), 'Public/Private: Gender, Social and Political Citizenship in Eastern Europe', paper presented at the Second ESA Conference, Budapest, Aug./Sept.

International Labour Orgnaisation (1998), *Women in Poverty: Evaluation of Politics and Strategies for Decrease of Poverty in Bulgaria*, Geneva: ILO Bulgaria: UNDP.

International Organization for Migration (1995), *Trafficking and Prostitution: The Growing Exploitation of Migrant Women from Central and Eastern Europe*, Budapest: Migration Information Programme.

Ivekovic, R. (1977), 'Women, Politics, Peace', in Kasic (1997), pp.95–108.

Jones, K. (1990), 'Citizenship in a Woman-friendly Polity', *Signs*, 15:781–812

Kasic, B. (1997), *Women and the Politics of Peace: Contributions to a Culture of Women's Resistance*, Zagreb: Centre for Women's Studies.

Khadzhiyski, I. (1974), *Bit i dushevnost na nashiya narod* [Lifestyle and Mentality of Our People], Sofia: Bulgarski pisatel.

Kolarska-Bobinska, L. (1990), 'The Myth of the Market and the Reality of Reform', in S. Gomulka and A. Polonsky (eds.), *Polish Paradoxes*, London: Routledge, pp.160–79.

Konrad, G. (1984), *Anti-Politics: An Essay*, London: Quartet.

Kumar, R. (1993), 'Introduction', in R. Kumar and J. Kaldor-Robinson (eds.), *Nationality and Citizenship: A Discussion*, Prague: Helsinki Citizens Assembly Publication Series 5.

Kristeva, J. (1986), 'Women's Time', in T. Moi (ed.), *The Kristeva Reader*, Oxford: Basil Blackwell.

Law on Political Parties (1994), *The Official Gazette of the Republic of Slovenia*, Ljubljana, 7 Oct.

Lentin, R. (ed.), *Gender and Catastrophe*, London: Zed Books.

Liborakina, M. (1977), 'Women and the Politics of Peace: Lessons Learned from the War in Chechnya', in Kasic (1997), pp.119–30.

Lissyutkina, Larisa (1993), 'Soviet Women at the Crossroads of Perestroika', in Funk and Mueller (eds.) (1993).

Lister, R. (1997), 'Citizenship: Towards a Feminist Synthesis'.

Lutz, H. (1997), 'The Limits of Europeanness: Immigrant Women in Fortress Europe', *Citizenship: Pushing the Boundaries, Feminist Review*, No.57 (1997) pp.93–111.

Lorde, A. (1996), *The Audre Lorde Compendium*, London: The Women's Press.

Marsh, R. (ed.) (1996), *Women in Russia and Ukraine*, Cambridge: Cambridge University Press.

Marshall, T.H. (1950/1992), 'Citizenship and Social Class', in T. Bottomore and T.H. Marshall, *Citizenship and Social Class*, London: Pluto Press.

Mertus, J. *et al.* (1997), *The Suitcase: Refugee Voices from Bosnia and Croatia*, Berkeley, CA: University of California Press.

Mladineo Desnica, M. (1996), 'Croatia: Three Years After', in Corrin (ed.) (1996), pp.133–6.
Mladjenovic, L. (1996), 'Dirty Streets', in Corrin (ed.) (1996), pp.27–30.
Mouffe, C. (ed.) (1992), *Dimensions of Radical Democracy: Pluralism, Citizenship, Community*, London: Verso.
National Assembly of 13 September 1994, Session Records, Ljublijana, Slovenia.
Offe, C. (1996), *Varieties of Transition: The East European and East German Experiences*, Cambridge: Polity.
Parker, A., Russo, M. Sommer, D. and P. Yaeger (eds.) (1992), *Nationalisms and Sexualities*, London: Routledge.
Pateman, C. (1988), *The Sexual Contract*, Cambridge: Polity Press.
Pateman, C. (1989), *The Disorder of Women*, Cambridge, Polity Press.
Pilkington, H. (ed.) (1996) *Gender, Generation and Identity in Contemporary Russia* London: Routledge.
Polish Committee of NGOs (1995), The Situation of Women in Poland: *Report of the NGOs Committee*, Warsaw: Polish Committee of NGOs Beijing.
Posadskaya, A. (ed.) (1994), *Women in Russia: A New Era in Russian Feminism*, London: Verso.
Rai, S., Pilkington, H. and A. Phizaklea (eds.) (1992), *Women in the Face of Change: The Soviet Union, Eastern Europe and China*, London: Routledge.
Reeves-Ellington, B. (1996), 'A Woman's Place in Bulgaria: Past Perspectives, Current Realities', paper presented to the National Women's Studies Association Conference, Skidmore College, New York, 12–16 June 1996.
Renne, T. (ed.) (1997), *Ana's Land: Sisterhood in Eastern Europe*, Boulder, CO and Oxford: Westview.
Rueschmeyer, M. (ed.) (1994), *Women in the Politics of Postcommunist Eastern Europe*, Armonk, NY and London: M.E. Sharpe.
Salamon, L.M., 'The Rise of the Nonprofit Sector', *Foreign Affairs*, July–Aug. 1994.
Scheppele, K.L. (1994), 'Rethinking Group Rights', unpublished paper.
Scott, J. (1988), 'Deconstructing Equality-versus-Difference: Or the Uses of Poststructuralist Theory for Feminism', *Feminist Studies*, Vol.14, No.1, pp.33–50.
Siklova, J. (1993), 'Are Women in Eastern and Central Europe Conservative?', in Funk and Mueller (eds.) (1993).
Slovene Statistical Yearbook, 1993.
Somers, M. (1992), 'Law, Community and Political Culture in the Transition to Democracy', *American Sociological Review* 58, pp.587–620.
Spivak, G. (1990), *The Post-Colonial Critic*, London: Routledge.
Stilglmayer, A. (ed.) (1994), *Mass Rape: The War against Women in Bosnia-Herzegovina*, Lincoln, NE: University of Nebraska Press.
True, J. (1994), 'Gendered Citizenship: "East-West" Comparisons in a Post-War Era', paper at IPSA conference, Berlin, Sept.
Suleri, S. (1991) 'Woman Skin Deep: Feminism and the Postcolonial Condition', *Critical Inquiry*, Vol.18, No.1.
Tomova, I. (1995), *The Gypsies in the Transition Period*, Sofia: International Center for Minority Studies and Intercultural Relations.
ULSD Congress Documents (1996), Ljubljana: Slovenj Gradec.
Women in Political Parties (1994), Ljubljana: Governmental Office for Women's Politics.
Yuval-Davis, N. (1997b), 'Women, Citizenship and Difference', Citizenship: Pushing the Boundaries, *Feminist Review* No.57, Autumn 1997, pp.4–27.
Zajc, D. (1993), 'Some Problems of Representation in the Process of Slovene Political Transition', unpublished paper.
Zajovic, S. (1992), 'Patriarchy, Language and National Myth', *Peace News*, March.
Zajovic, S. (ed.) (1997), *Women for Peace*, Belgrade: Women in Black.
Zajovic, S. (1997), 'In Her Own Name (Cassandra's Principle)', in Kasic (1997), pp.31–4.

compiled by Chris Corrin

Index

Books of Related Interest

Beyond Stalinism:
Communist Political Evolution

Ronald J. Hill (Ed)

'Evolution' has taken place both *within* and *from communism*. Both of these aspects of communist political evolution are examined in this volume of essays by leading British and Scandinavian students of communism and communist systems, who elaborate the concept and apply it to specific cases.

180 pages   1999
0 7146 3463 8 cloth

The Soviet Transition:
From Gorbachev to Yeltsin

Stephen White, Rita di Leo and Ottorino Cappelli (Eds)

The dramatic transition from Soviet Communism to a democratic Russia has been one of the landmark events of the twentieth century. In this volume a group of leading students of Soviet and post-Soviet affairs, drawn from western Europe and the former Soviet Union itself, examine the transition from Gorbachev to Yeltsin in its variety and complexity.

240 pages   1999
0 7146 4528 1 cloth

FRANK CASS PUBLISHERS
Newbury House, 900 Eastern Avenue, Ilford, Essex, IG2 7HH
Tel: +44 (0)181 599 8866 Fax: +44 (0)181 599 0984 E-mail: info@frankcass.com
NORTH AMERICA
5804 NE Hassalo Street, Portland, OR 97213 3644, USA
Tel: 800 944 6190 Fax: 503 280 8832 E-mail: cass@isbs.com
Website: www.frankcass.com

Social Democracy in a Post-Communist Europe

**Michael Waller, Bruno Coppieters and
Kris Deschouwer (Eds)**

This book examines the fortunes of social democracy since 1989 in the
former GDR, Poland, Hungary, the Czech Republic and Slovakia,
setting that analysis in a broader European framework, and relating the
current problems of social democracy in western Europe to
developments in the east of the continent.

216 pages 1999
0 7146 4552 2 cloth
0 7146 4092 1 paper

Post-Communism and the Media in Eastern Europe

Patrick H. O'Neil (Ed)

This study, an investigation of the media in Poland, the Czech Republic,
Slovakia, Hungary, Romania and Bulgaria by American and East
European scholars, seeks to outline both the general legacies of
communism that confront media reform in eastern Europe, as well as
point to how the specific interaction between the media, state, society
and market has led to the development of particular and unique
dynamics in each case.

144 pages 1999
0 7146 4765 9 cloth
0 7146 4311 4 paper

FRANK CASS PUBLISHERS
Newbury House, 900 Eastern Avenue, Ilford, Essex, IG2 7HH
Tel: +44 (0)181 599 8866 Fax: +44 (0)181 599 0984 E-mail: info@frankcass.com
NORTH AMERICA
5804 NE Hassalo Street, Portland, OR 97213 3644, USA
Tel: 800 944 6190 Fax: 503 280 8832 E-mail: cass@isbs.com
Website: www.frankcass.com

Parties, Trade Unions and Society in East-Central Europe

Michael Waller and Martin Myant

In this volume the relationship between political parties and trade unions in Poland, the Czech Republic, Slovakia, Hungary and Bulgaria is analysed. The work is the collective product of a number of publicly-funded research projects devoted to the process of change in eastern Europe and of some of their East European collaborators.

184 pages   1999
0 7146 4583 4   cloth

FRANK CASS PUBLISHERS
Newbury House, 900 Eastern Avenue, Ilford, Essex, IG2 7HH
Tel: +44 (0)181 599 8866 Fax: +44 (0)181 599 0984 E-mail: info@frankcass.com
NORTH AMERICA
5804 NE Hassalo Street, Portland, OR 97213 3644, USA
Tel: 800 944 6190 Fax: 503 280 8832 E-mail: cass@isbs.com
Website: www.frankcass.com